„ Książki są lekarstwem
dla umysłu "
　　　　　Demokryt

Dominiko , niech ta książka
będzie również lekarstwem dla
Twojego ciała ☺

　　Wszystkiego najlepszego
　z okazji urodzin
　　　życzą:
　Magda, Krystian, Emilia
　　i Tymoteusz
Bruni's Snow Bowl Hut 4 sierpnia 2023r.

WILD DRINKS

The new old world of
small-batch brews, ferments
and infusions

SHARON FLYNN

Hardie Grant

BOOKS

The bubbles in these drinks are quite wild, but they willingly come together in your kitchen to make that slightly sour, lightly fizzy soda, kombucha, kvass, kefir, cider, mead, beer or wine. Sometimes within days, but often a bit longer. We are so used to buying these drinks ready-made that you wouldn't be blamed for not thinking about where the bubbles come from. We mix drinks, we don't make them. Yet it's so easy to encourage effervescence from water and simple ingredients - all with tools you already have in your kitchen. The bonus is that downing a delicious living drink is also an easy way to get the good bugs into your gut - and your life - naturally. We are mostly water and microbial cells ourselves, so it makes sense to drink water you've grown life into.

Most of these recipes have been shared over generations; they have morphed into different forms around the world but you can see their connections. I want these recipes to inspire you to brew, infuse and ferment from your pantry, garden, market or store. To go foraging, to stir and nurture, taste and imagine and then quietly sip or proudly share what you've made. Creating your own wild drinks will connect you to our shared human experience of the power and magic of a good brew.

A wink from the invisible can lighten the mundanity of our everyday. Fermenting brings that magic - that life - back into a kitchen; a place that is usually the end point for what was living. I hope your hands delve into this life, and that it feeds your curiosity as well as you and your people. And: wild drinks are very tasty, too. Enjoy.

CONTENTS

WILD SODA WITH POMEGRANATE

INTRODUCTION

Perhaps the best way to appreciate a thing is to learn to make it yourself, even just once. Not only for the joy, empowerment and independence a new skill can provide, but also to gain an appreciation of the time it takes to master that skill. Once you delve into something a bit deeper – from scratch – you see rays of awe and wonder shining from the small everyday things. Which then, in my experience, leads to delving further. There is always so much to discover.

If you're lucky, nothing is more everyday than eating and drinking. Most of us grow up learning about food in an intimate, hands-on way: eating, watching, helping with, and eventually, making our own food. Even if we haven't cooked for ourselves at all, we have seen someone doing it at home and understand the relationship between heat and the transformation it effects in our food. When it comes to drinks, few of us have experienced them as makers; rather, we experience them as consumers. Or, for those more interested, as voyeurs. From the dabblers to the very serious, going to a tasting, a vineyard, a brewery or distillery to sample the drink and learn about the maker, the region and the processes is fun.

We tend to think of drinks in a different way to our food. But beverages have been bottled and sold and then shipped off to far places long before packaged foods ever were, and they were perhaps among the first products to be scaled, taxed and traded. It's a perfect market as they are consumed quickly, can be intoxicating and, like coffee, also addictive. Some people reflect on and are captivated by the source, particularly in the case of drinks containing alcohol. There are qualifications and shelves of books dedicated to the 'terroir' and the importance of place, water, soil, technique, tradition and heritage. Yet it seems to occur to very few people that they could have a go at making, brewing or fermenting their own ancient drinks.

Stirring water into honey for a sparkling mead, smashing fruit to turn to wine, using bread for a simple beer, whey for a fizzy quick soda or fruit scraps and water for vinegar – it's all pretty easy, cheap and fun. It's also full of good living stuff your gut will benefit from. Most home brews are delicious, although I warn you that you'll certainly make some that aren't (just as with home-cooked food). The taste of 'the hand' is the flavour of home that rings through and calls us back. I think this is even more so with the subtle nuance, seasonality and gentle effervescence in a homemade drink.

Many of us like to play with the microscopic world for our own eating and drinking pleasure. Fermenting and brewing your own drinks is easier than baking sourdough bread, cheesemaking or meat curing. Making kombucha and kefir is certainly not much more complicated than fermenting vegetables to make pickles, sauerkraut and kimchi. Humans have relied on these methods forever, calling on wild bacteria and fungi. Life living in balance naturally – on, within and all around us. We've relied upon it in our kitchens and, in the case of drinks, to help make water safer to drink, to preserve produce, to make medicines from plants, alcohol from sugars, and sometimes as a pathway to something more mystical or spiritual. We managed to pass our recipes down through generations, and people found ways to make them.

Homemade is always seen as healthier and, in the case of drinks, the natural bacteria and yeasts that thrive during the fermentation process have now been found to be beneficial – a probiotic. You can preserve a season in a bottle and, on top of that, the drinks you make at home can be simultaneously good for your gut and your spirit. Drinks are an easy sell to friends and family – much easier, I have found, than getting them to add vegetable ferments to their diet. The drinks you find in your supermarket just won't compare. In order to scale, the drink needs to have a long shelf life, to be stable, predictable and reliable. Most home brews – particularly the wild ones – have fizz aplenty and every batch is different. They often need to be kept in the fridge and have a fairly short shelf life.

HOW THE FERMENTARY WAS BORN

For one reason or another I have always moved. I lived in Malaysia and Denmark as a teen, in Japan for much of my twenties, and then moved with my children over to Chicago, Seattle, Brussels and finally back to Australia, eventually landing in Melbourne. No matter where, I have always been attracted to the foods that I later learnt came under the umbrella of fermentation. In fact, I have been fermenting all kinds of things from all over the world since my early twenties. Longer kitchen projects like fermenting were a comfort, familiar, a routine amid so much moving. The commitment and the act of growing and tending to something was like company for me. A bubble here, an overflow there – a reaction, a fizz. Life on my bench that I knew. We spoke to each other.

Predictably, each new place came with so many new flavours, foods and traditions to learn from. But also, and quite importantly, new audiences to share my concoctions with – to convert a fussy palate or captivate a tired one. Drinks are a very easy way to start rewilding a gut; to get the medicine down, Mary Poppins style. But there are certain recipes in this book that changed the direction of my life altogether.

At the end of our time in Brussels, my youngest daughter caught what seemed like a normal cold, but it turned into something that led to a long period of taking a variety of antibiotics that left her sicker and in a very different place to where we'd started. A bit lost and wondering what to do next, and in the thick of another move, I learnt about the direct connection between living foods and drinks, our precious and vulnerable microbiome and its own very real connection to our brain and moods.

By living foods I mean yoghurt, sauerkraut, nattō, kimchi, brine-pickled anything, kefirs and the like. Foods that haven't been pasteurised and still have bacteria growing and living in them. Or foods that have been fermented, so they're easier to digest. If you've ever looked after someone quite unwell, with no plan or end in sight, you'll understand how vulnerable you can become and, hence, how empowering and transformative it was to have a focus, to be active in my daughter's healing and contribute toward her wellness. And to have some hope.

Upon moving back to Australia, I happened upon milk kefir grains – I was already aware of milk kefir but had only had the store-bought kind. Making my own was a whole different thing. Then I tried water kefir grains, bought a book on gut health and set up my kitchen with a simple plan: to fix Lucia's microbiome through food the best I could, with the time I had. No surprise, the drinks were not only the easiest to make but the easiest to serve and certainly the most popular. They were like a soda (which was formerly only for special occasions). And soon, after adding ferments rather than taking food away, Lulu went from only wanting simple carbohydrates to craving sour. Her gut started to appreciate a new democracy and she started requesting the drinks I made in the morning as well – visibly relishing the sour, fermented drinks as well as those ferments on her plate, just a little bit with every meal.

At a new school, with a new community, I became a little evangelical, talking about fermenting and handing ferments out to anyone that showed an ounce of interest. Within months, I had five fridges in the garage full of water kefir, plus an honesty jar, and almost couldn't brew fast enough. I would deliver brews and ferments to anyone on the choir and sport route, and I tried to teach people to just

make their own. But they usually didn't want to. They were afraid of working with bacteria and didn't really have the confidence, the space, and more importantly, the will. So I took the cash, continued filling up vats and fridges and kept peddling from the car. I felt dangerous and underground like I never had before. About a year later, I was fully embedded and focused on making beautiful ferments.

The Fermentary was born through the healing of my daughter's gut because I needed good, living ferments. I reasoned that if there were butchers and bakers, cheesemongers, specialty tea shops and, indeed, pharmacies, then there should be local fermentaries. And that it would be my goal to share this almost lost tradition as well as I could. Because to make your own small-batch flavours and living foods, to skip the queue of the mass-produced is a revolt, a revolution. This reversion to the unhomogenised, slower, localised and handcrafted is part of the rewilding that we sorely need – in our food system, in our bodies and in all of the places that have been subject to the industrialised food system.

In writing this book focusing on drinks, I found a connection between my own journey of making drinks and the women throughout history who have brewed from their homes to generate extra income to support a household, just as I had. I brewed to help my daughter's gut, then for a community of people, and in so doing I began to supplement an income which became a real business with a team, orders to fill and rent to pay.

Making drinks will bring magic into your kitchen in a bit of a witchy, apothecary, homesteading way. I still brew at home. To use up fruit, excess from a neighbour or farmer, to make a herbal healing brew, to entice a tired mind or gut with something good and refreshing – or simply to feed my own curiosity.

Not only can you brew kombucha and kefir in your kitchen, but you can brew beers, sake, makgeolli, kvass, cider, mead and all kinds of sodas. You can easily make sparkling soda out of everyday herbs, flowers, fruit and vegetables, or syrups to flavour your drinks. And you can make delicious treats from the by-products of these drinks. Wild drinks don't need to be made in large amounts. You don't need to brew twenty litres at a time (as you may have seen in sheds around the place). Small batches are good enough and mean you can get creative without too much risk and effort. Brewing this way is more fun and flexible. Nurture, grow, infuse, ferment – enjoy! It's what we are made of. Microbes are our own nature.

Early on in my fermenting adventure, I aimed to simply teach people how to ferment for themselves but many were quite unwell and were seeking a cure. They wanted a prescription. To talk to someone. To be told it would work. Without fail, after every workshop someone would ask me how much they should 'take'.

I would explain that these ferments are simply traditional foods and drinks that we'd mostly been missing out on for just a few generations. Yes, they're living drinks, filled with beneficial bacteria, with complex flavours, and they're a total departure from the highly processed foods we've been offered for years. Yes, it's good to start consuming them in small amounts, quite slowly if your system is very sensitive. Yes, be patient and listen to your body, trust your intuition and use common sense. But this is food after all. Food and drink. Not to be taken, but to be enjoyed.

I also hope that people learn that a relaxed gut is important in the healing process. Breathe - eat and drink slowly - at a table. Love yourself. You can't heal a gut by taking a mouthful of sauerkraut once a week, here and there, because what goes in also goes out - of course it does! Feed yourself well, including small amounts of a wide variety of fermented foods and drinks regularly!

HOW TO USE THIS BOOK

The recipes in this book are a guide; this is not the same as baking a cake. Wild fermentation is unconstrained, untamed, sometimes unpredictable. As such, amounts given in many recipes can be slightly adjusted to suit your taste, and some ingredient volumes are an approximation rather than an exact measurement (handfuls, for instance). Take the recipes as a starting point and experiment. It takes practice and patience before you'll achieve the results you expect. I hope that with my help and guidance, you'll get a very good drink the very first time because I've made the mistakes for you, and my recipes work. This is a collection of many years of drink-making; the recipes are the result of a lot of tinkering observations, tastings, travel, reading, conversations and research. But keep in mind: sometimes, even the most predictable recipes don't go as planned, and in wild fermentation, that's even more likely.

Have a flip through the book and start with whatever draws you in, or something that perhaps you have been curious about or that suits your available time. Maybe you don't have a SCOBY (symbiotic culture of bacteria and yeast) – so start with a wild soda or mead. All of the drinks in this book are achievable to the beginner, and they come from a place and a time where they were made in more rustic environments and with more basic tools than what we have today so it's not out of reach no matter what equipment you have or don't have (for information on fermenting equipment and considerations, see the Nurture chapter, page 13).

The grain drinks in the Brew chapter (page 35) are the least seasonal. Some, like the sake or makgeolli, require a bit more patience and can tie you to more of a schedule. Remember, all fermentation requires time, some nurturing and growing, so if you don't have those things right now, just head straight to Infuse (page 165), where you'll find syrups, teas and all kinds of old ways to preserve abundant fruits and botanicals.

The Ferment chapter (page 89) is where you can pick, chop, squash and let the magic happen with nothing more than produce from the greengrocer, farmers' market, or verge and roadside stalls.

You'll find drinks that require you to grow and feed something – usually a culture – in the Feed and Grow chapter (page 127). For some of them, you need to acquire a culture, mother or SCOBY. Be prepared for an ongoing relationship here. The vinegars are where you can go if you have let a brew go too far or have a lot of herbs – the vinegar recipes extend into the Infuse chapter (page 165).

For ways to use spent ingredients and for extensions of a few of the ferments that aren't only for consumption, look at the Enjoy chapter (page 197). You'll find that in your wild drink making, you'll get a lot of excess lees and grains, for example, and you'll want different ways to serve or enjoy them – as not only frugal but satisfying products on their own.

Your kitchen might well become a cross between a herbalist's greenhouse, an

apothecary, a brewery and a grain store. Brewing and fermenting is easy, and we can all learn the skills involved – to percolate, feed, infuse, impart, filter, steep, rise and grow. In this fast world, perhaps the waiting and listening is the hardest part of all. It'll be worth it. You'll see.

This book uses 20 ml (¾ fl oz) tablespoons and 250 ml (8½ fl oz) cup measures.

'Your kitchen might well become a cross between a herbalist's greenhouse, an apothecary, a brewery and a grain store.'

Nurture

NURTURE

ON WILD FERMENTATION

To get your own living foods and drinks growing, the most important components are simple: time, the right ingredients and environment, trusting your senses and your innate intuition, and certainly an element of hope and curiosity.

Wild fermenting can provide your kitchen and food life with a sense of time and place, a call to milk the seasons for things when they are plentiful. It can require some routine and care that, at times, may feel as demanding as a pet. But once you are into a rhythm, you will find the continuity, expectation and waiting to be quite comforting. Close a vessel with a piece of cloth or a lid, check it, stir or don't, wait and listen for nature to do the work – for the unseen to feed and deposit. Your job is to set up an environment the microbes love and to let nature's intellect be your guide.

Natural fermentation, throughout the world, and in our collective past, from hunter-gatherer to urbanised society, has been used to transform many of our favourite foods. It has made previously inedible ingredients delicious, has made foods easier to digest and more nutritious, and most certainly has created a more complex, longer flavour. More importantly, it has been a reliable way to preserve food that is in abundance.

These days, live fermented foods have become less abundant in our homes, yet more and more research into our gut-brain axis and our microbiome indicates that consuming living bacteria and yeasts can be beneficial and promotes a healthier immune system. Inside and out, we have been sorely lacking in microbial life. We've learnt how looking after that life plays an important part in how the rest of our body functions – even as far as to how we feel and think. Our gut is our second brain.

Maybe you are already a maker or drinker of one of the ancient brews making a modern comeback: sparkling mead, milk kefir, water kefir, wild soda, sake or makgeolli. If so, you'll know that all fermentation naturally results in a small amount of residual alcohol, in some drinks

LET'S TALK ABOUT YEAST AND BACTERIA

The word ferment comes from the Latin fervere - to boil. While there is heat in a ferment, the bubbles we see in fermentation obviously aren't boiling. These gassy bubbles are the sign of bacteria at work.

Before microscopes enabled us to see microbes at work, there was mystery around the bubbles and reactions in our ferments. Different yeasts each have their lifestyle preferences: what temperatures they thrive in, what they like to eat, where they hang out (bottom or top of vessel, floating around in the air, sitting and waiting around for the skin on fruit to break open, for instance). Before yeasts were seen and understood scientifically, we called upon them through superstition, ritual and spiritual and cultural acts employing sound and energy, such as dancing and singing loudly, or using certain tools on a certain day, for example, to bring the magic to the brew.

Antonie van Leeuwenhoek first observed yeast; later, Louis Pasteur declared yeast to be an actual living creature. He discovered fermentation brought about two main results: alcohols and acids (lactic and acetic). In general, yeast is responsible for alcohol, and bacteria mostly for the acids.

Yeasts are members of the fungus world, which includes our lovely moulds as well. Different yeasts have different tolerances for alcohol. Wild yeasts are the ones we catch naturally - they live in and on us, in the soil and on the vegetables and fruit we put into our ferments. In a wild ferment, yeasts make the alcohol while, simultaneously, the bacteria make the environment more acidic. As the acidity and the alcohol levels change, so do the types of life in your ferment. At a certain level, the environment gets intolerable for some bacteria and yeasts and they die. With a wild ferment, after a point, no more alcohol is produced as the natural yeasts don't tolerate alcohol levels of more than 12% ABV (alcohol by volume). Look at page 29 to learn more about measuring alcohol in your brews.

You can also buy packets of yeast that have been developed for a specific flavour or alcohol level. These are available online and in home brewing stores and you can learn which yeast is good for what quite easily.

Lactobacillus is a genus of bacteria that make up much of the microbiome in our bodies. You'll see them as LAB (lactic acid bacteria). The lactic has nothing to do with milk; LAB dwell in and love all of our ferments. Recent studies into our gut-brain connection and gut health in general are finding certain species of bacteria are particularly good for us. In a wild ferment, you are likely to get a diverse range of bacteria, which is what we are after. With our food industry relying on proprietary yeasts, our foods and drinks all contain the same small number of microbes when, in fact, there are many, many more kinds out there. It is desirable to have a wide variety of bacteria in our foods - it's what our bodies and our soil seek. The world is much more interesting and varied than just those things that are grown for profit in a laboratory. A wild ferment, for the most part, tends to kick out any unwanted bacteria. If it didn't, how would we be here now? We have evolved alongside them.

more than in others. Considering the life in the drink, I prefer to think of them as 'functional' rather than just in terms of alcoholic versus non-alcoholic. There is a big difference between a cordial with water and a living ferment that is brimming with life and natural bubbles (and therefore, life that will feed your gut). Perhaps consider, too, that the small amount of alcohol also has the function of relaxing the gut, providing a longer flavour and better mouthfeel. Alcohol has a function here – yeasts turn sugar into carbon dioxide and alcohol before it goes into acetic acid. Even the liquid from our sauerkraut has about 1% alcohol. We aren't fermenting with alcohol as our goal, but it is a part of the cycle of fermentation. Keep that in mind.

WATER

Most of the drinks in this book rely on water. While water quality can affect your brews, as a dabbler or beginner, the main thing to worry about is that your tap water isn't highly chlorinated. If it is, sit it overnight in an open container to evaporate some of the chemical.

Filtered rainwater is a fabulous option – my favourite. It's soft already, free and sustainable; my water kefir grains have always thrived on it.

Natural springs provide pure water that is likely to be rich in iron, calcium and other minerals and is great for fermenting with; if you have a spring nearby – go for it.

Using activated charcoal filters to filter impurities from water will provide a neutral base for brewing, and they are easy enough to source. So too are the purifiers based on movement, with water running through a ceramic filter and over rocks and stones, for example.

Distilled water has been vaporised and is devoid of life, which we don't really want, but it can be good to dilute very rich waters or to add to wine when you're making vinegar, for example.

Bore or well water is not usually recommended for brewers as it is quite hard; however, adding a water softener will help.

INGREDIENTS

Most of the ingredients suggested for these often ancient recipes are readily available from shops, markets or networks, or can be sourced online. Some of the ingredients can be a little harder to source as we tend to have a very limited selection of herbs and roots available in most mainstream supermarkets and greengrocers these days. Asian food stores are great for small packets of dried roots that you would never see in a regular supermarket. Try them out – look them up and think about

how you might put them in a drink. A lot of our ferments are seen as functional – and the acid in a drink often makes the nutrients in dried herbs more accessible and powerful.

Foraging or growing your own is one way of sourcing ingredients. Many of the herbs used for brewing are hardy and great for beginner growers as well. I found I needed these ingredients and flavours so frequently that I began to grow my own, which was a wonderful segue from kitchen bench microbe grower into a passionate, obsessive gardener, worrying about microbes in soil and learning to care for more than I imagined. This is a sensible direction to go in if you are fermenting a lot.

Not all the ingredients are ones you'll want to grow. Things that are seen as weeds by many appear frequently in the old brew recipes: dandelions, mugwort, nettles, burdock and wormwood, chamomile and borage, spruce, birch and many others. Most were used because they were readily available, easy to forage for or save; many are still easy to find. Perhaps you'll find only a few and collect them in the freezer until you have enough.

These botanicals also provide yeasts, bitterness and preserving agents, not to mention their medicinal properties, all of which are things I love in my brew. Sometimes you need a lot of them – like in Dandelion wine (page 96) – but for the most part, these herbs and botanicals are only needed in small amounts because they are often quite potent.

EXPERIMENTATION

Working with wild fermentation is not an exact science. There are countless variations and part of the fun is the experimenting, the observing, the learning.

Actively keep a notebook and record your methods and results: use different ingredients,

GARLIC DRYING, AND RHUBARB READY FOR FIZZING

dried or fresh; try varieties of grain; explore soaking and drying times, sprouting and cooking methods, yeast types, temperature and fermentation time, vessel types, water. The journey is as enjoyable as the destination.

You really don't need much specialised equipment to play with most of the recipes in this book. Sometimes, specialist equipment and gadgets intimidate people and get in the way of creativity, so don't go too far out of your way for things you don't need. A bit of MacGyver ingenuity and flexibility is desirable too.

Remember that our ancestors did not rely on much more than their experience and their senses – the feel, smell, taste and activity. So can you. You can judge temperature with your body, or measure alcohol by mouthfeel. You can smell yeast and alcohol, taste sweet and sour and don't really need to know what

the pH is exactly, nor predict where the alcohol is going all the time. But as my friend in fermenting, Holly Davis, says: 'You can never learn less', so with that in mind, for precision in your ferments, do measure if you like, and take notes because this can often bring clarity when problem-solving.

FUNDAMENTALS

There are a few important factors for a good ferment:

- clean equipment
- vessels and lids appropriate to the ferment
- the right temperature

These elements aren't difficult to achieve or find but need to be considered for every ferment. Review these factors in your notes if you have a failed batch.

SETTING UP THE RIGHT ENVIRONMENT

STERILISATION

Rather than hope for a sterile environment, aim for a sanitised one. Complete sterilisation in a home kitchen is very difficult, but we do need to limit unwanted microbes in our brews. So always make sure your hands, tools, work area, bowls, tubes, fermenters and bottles, lids and seals – all the things that will come in contact with your brew along the way – are all as clean as possible.

A good wash in hot soapy water, plus a rinse in very hot water, is recommended. I find it useful to have a 10 litre (2.6 gallon) tub to store everything in when I'm not brewing which I then use on brewing day – filled with water and the sanitiser of choice so I can dip, soak or rinse things as I go.

If your bottles are new or only lightly soiled, a hot whirl in the dishwasher works fine; you can fill straight from the dishwasher rack.

No-rinse spray sanitisers are available at home brew stores and online, as are concentrates you can dilute into a bucket to soak your equipment in. Just follow the directions on the container. It's great to be able to use the no-rinse style in a container or bucket of water to clean lids and bottles and to push the water through your tubing and bottling gun.

I love a good bottle brush and have them in all sizes. For older bottles, you can find beads especially for washing bottles, and decanters to really clean the bottom; then use a good strong bottle brush as well. This is particularly relevant if you are using second-hand bottles and don't know what's been in them. You can buy various bottle trees to hold the bottles upside down to dry, or line a sink or tub with a towel and place them upside down to drip dry, only turning them over at bottling.

FERMENTATION VESSELS

For certain recipes, it's preferable to have at least two fermentation vessels so you can manage your first and second ferment – one for the fermentation to begin and another for the strained liquid to be flavoured and to carbonate. You can find many variations of glass jars and bottles, large fermenters, ceramic crocks and pots once you start looking. In fact, there are many very beautiful ferment- and brew-related bits and pieces you can acquire with the passage of time, and finding these is a real pleasure.

Uncomplicated vessels without lots of nooks, crannies and corners are easier to clean and fundamentally stronger. Corners are weak spots and when you are working with gases a weak spot means explosions and breakages. Be a bit wary of fancy decorative pots and glass jars as they may contain lead in the paint or glaze. Likewise, plastic containers need to be food grade and BPA-free.

Thick glass is perfect for your brews and easy to find. I love the darker glass – brown and green – but regular is fine, and I reiterate: thick glass and mostly round is safest and best.

encourage the necessary bacteria and yeast to settle and later inoculate your ferment or brew. Traditionally, we relied on this as a support – almost a starter culture in itself. Make sure any ceramic glaze is food safe (no lead).

Stainless steel is great for fermenting in, but the vats mostly come in very large sizes. We do use them for fermenting large quantities of vegetables and drinks and a most useful feature is the variable lid: whether you fill the vat or only half-fill it, you can push the lid down close to the level of the brew or ferment. When it comes to metal, stick with stainless steel as it is non-reactive and will last for years.

LIDS, COVERINGS AND AIRLOCK SYSTEMS

You will require different types of lids depending on the ferment. Ferments that are aerobic – requiring exposure to the air – just need to be covered loosely with cloth, and the cloth needs to be secured to keep the drink clean and bug-free. This is critical with kombucha and vinegar. I keep large swathes of cotton and muslin (cheesecloth) (page 30) on hand and have varying sizes of them ready to use.

Other drinks require a sealable lid that also allows the gases formed in the brew to escape. One method is simply burping a regular lidded vessel. It's exactly as it sounds: you release the lid from time to time to expel the carbon dioxide. A jar with a flip-top lid and rubber ring is good for this as it will leach a little naturally and is easy to flick open and close quickly.

An easier method – one that requires no burping and that gives a more predictable and delicious result – is using an airlock system.

Airlocks

An airlock lid system allows the gases formed during fermentation to escape immediately while simultaneously keeping air

A carboy, also known as a demijohn, is a larger glass bottle or jug with or without handles or handle attachments designed for fermenting, ageing or storing your brew in. They come in a variety of sizes (commonly 5–23 L/1–6 gallon), neck sizes and with different openings and lidding systems. A glass carboy is fairly standard in a brewing kit. Beware of the super large vessels because once you fill them, they are very heavy and might end up staying where you filled them!

Ceramic vessels and wooden barrels are my favourite. They both provide an earthy and breathable atmosphere that is porous enough to

Misc. Glass Jars

out. They are a fabulous tool for anaerobic fermentation (fermenting without oxygen present). You'll use them for fermenting vegetables as well.

Most airlocks are like an S bend – you pour a small amount of water into the 's', making sure it is in both channels. The gas will bubble out but the water will stop any air or other unwanted particles or airborne yeasts from entering and spoiling your brew. Having an airlock that utilises water not only helps you keep your ferment safe, but it is also quite 'communicative' in that you can hear the bubbles (a very pleasant sound) and know how active your brew is. You'll usually know a brew is ready when the airlock only bubbles once every couple of minutes, or if it is picking up on a hot day and bubbling like crazy. It's a really great way to know what is going on.

Many demijohns come with the choice of a lid or a rubber stopper and airlock. I have both: using the airlock for primary fermenting and the lid for storing or secondary fermenting. Bottles also do well with a simple balloon that will catch the gas and let you know what's going on in there. It's fun to watch the balloon fill (see page 116).

If you are making your own airlock you'll need a rubber bung or something to line the hole with. If you have ordinary large jars, just drill a hole in the lid and slot the airlock and bung in there. Another really good, easy makeshift way is to just use a tube – like a siphon tube – as the airlock; put it into your bottle or jar, making sure it's tight and no other air gets in or out around the tube. Then put the other end into a bucket or jar filled with water. It will bubble away nicely and look rather curious.

There are other airlock systems on the market now; a silicone nipple is quite popular too. Going to a home brew store will help clarify all of these options for you.

TEMPERATURE

WAYS TO COOL AND HEAT

Ambient temperatures can make a big difference to flavour in fermenting. Higher temperatures can create acetone or overly fruity flavours. If it's too warm, you can also get a sour brew through the encouragement of too much lactobacillus early on. Acetone (which emits the distinct smell of nail polish remover) may mean yeast such as pichia is present. This can be avoided by aeration – make sure to stir often in the first couple of days and keep your brew or ferment in a place that has plenty of fresh air.

A cool air temperature can make the fermentation long and slow, but in many cases this results in a delicious, more complex result. But too cool and not much will happen, so you are aiming for a temperature above 8°C (46°F) most of the time. In general, fermentation best takes place at a room temperature of between 14–21°C (57–70°F) – but it depends on what you are fermenting, of course. Kombucha likes a higher temperature of 24–31°C (75–88°F).

A cool water or ice bath is a simple way of cooling something down, and you could add ice cubes to your brew if that suits as well. (This is more likely needed when you are brewing something thick with grains, such as sake – see page 67 – rather than most of the other brews in this book.)

An esky (icebox/cooler) with hot water bottles or ice packs is useful and versatile for heating and cooling. While I haven't relied on an immersion heater, plenty of people do. You could also look into that. An old fridge can also be hooked up to help incubate or keep cool, as can a wine fridge. I've also got a few different-sized thermal flasks that smaller jars fit into, as well as a couple of units designed for yoghurt making.

WAYS TO INCUBATE: KEEPING TEMPERATURE

Incubation relies on the steady control of ferment-friendly temperature, coupled with the right degree of humidity. The idea of a heat source with a humidifier (see below) sounds high-tech but it can be delightfully low-tech. It can be as basic as a bowl of water over a heat pad in a lidded plastic tub. Other useful incubators are an esky (icebox/cooler) or an insulated bag, plus the heat source (hot water bottles, electric blanket) with the addition of some moisture.

We have a small plastic greenhouse with a couple of shelves and a zip door that is quite perfect for brews of all shapes and sizes. When required, I add a heat mat and/or a humidifier on the ground. We use it for kombucha in winter and for anything else that needs that perfect sweet spot for growing healthy fungus. We use another year-round for growing mushrooms, and another for the seedlings I have started collecting. But, you can make an incubator out of anything.

My first incubator for kōji was very basic and worked beautifully. It was simply fashioned out of a long, thin and quite shallow plastic box meant for under-the-bed storage. I wrapped an electric blanket around it and lay a damp towel on the inner bottom of the box, with the kōji in glass and ceramic casserole dishes on top with a layer of cheesecloth to keep it from drying out. It worked. The inside of the lid needed wiping every now and then before it got drippy. I fussed a bit and checked a lot, but it worked.

Our current incubator is an old locker – lined with silver insulation paper – and very beautifully laid with cedar shelves for my handmade cedar- and celery-wood boxes. Inside it I have a humidifier, a humidity measure and a thermometer with alarms set for when they reach the too high or too low zone. Even with this fabulous safety net I like to keep an eye on how things are going and growing though. It also must be said – temperature and humidity controls aside – the main thing I use are my senses: smelling for the sweetness and the grapefruity, musky lovely aroma, checking the grains for moisture, and seeing how the mould is going. That beats all of the probes I have – they could be telling me numbers, but the aroma says it all.

Humidifier and humidity measure
There are loads of off-the-shelf humidifiers for sale. I bought one from an aquarium store. I recommend that you get a fairly small one because you will likely want to use it inside another chamber, such as a styrofoam box or esky (icebox/cooler). But if you're making your own, you are really only trying to make a chamber that retains a basic level of inherent or added moisture.

A humidity measure, also called a hygrometer, is a useful instrument to measure the moisture level in your fermentation set-up. There are all sorts of models available, some with alarm settings. Most have digital displays that can also be controlled via an app on your phone.

Bread proofing boxes
Another fabulous technology that I recommend. There are a few models that are foldable and

easy to store away, but won't fit very large items. You could also fashion your own with a similar container and a heat mat – there are plenty of online guides on how to make your own.

Yoghurt makers and other water agents
They can be an easy way of keeping a temperature. My latest yoghurt maker utilises a water bath that fits a 2 litre (68 fl oz/8 cups) jar inside. I use it for making yoghurt, and growing yeast and nattō. Water retains heat well. Take advantage of this fact by using an immersion cooker, sous vide system or steam oven, or a simple set-up of styrofoam boxes or a cooler with hot water bottles. A regular oven on very low, with your container sitting in a roasting tray of warm water, will also work.

Dehydrators
A dehydrator that has room for some water on the bottom also works as an incubator for times when you require humidity. You'll need to work out how to keep moisture in – cloth or plastic wrap do the job just fine.

Dehydrators come in handy in general. You can use them to dry grain for flours, cultures for storage or sharing, or to dehydrate spent fruit or other ingredients to grind into powders. I prefer dehydrators with a door and shelves over round models. I find the latter a bit more awkward to use, and it is harder to see how things are coming along.

FERMENTATION ACCESSORIES

SCALES

It's nice to be able to measure things right down to the gram when adding spores, so look for a digital kitchen scale like the ones used in coffee brewing.

PH METER OR STRIPS

Recording pH levels is a great learning tool – especially handy when you are looking for reasons something went wrong. It's advisable if you are doing big batches or making something that needs to be a certain acidity. You might also want to check whether your water is acidic or alkaline before you use it, or keep an eye on your ferments as they change. An electronic pH meter is better than the strips for sure; it's easier to use and gives a much more precise reading.

WINE THIEF OR BASTER

This wine trade device is a long, thin pipette to take some of the liquid out of a batch to sample without disturbing the whole thing. Most kitchen basters are quite a bit thicker so just make sure it will fit into the neck of your bottle or fermenter.

MEASURING SPOONS, CUPS AND JUGS

Have a good range of these measures in various sizes. When you only need a tiny drop, I recommend a syringe – have a very small one and a larger one on hand – for precision. Often, I will bottle up a dozen plain water kefir and squeeze 10 ml (¼ fl oz/about a tablespoon) of syrup per litre (34 fl oz/4 cups) into each using a syringe.

THERMOMETER

You'll need a food-grade thermometer. There are point-and-shoot styles that work beautifully, stickers to go on the side of a jar, or the type used for jams and candy making or yoghurt and cheeses. These are easy enough to find and not very expensive.

MEASURING ALCOHOL AND USING HERBS WITH CAUTION

Trace amounts of alcohol serve different functions in our brews: alcohol is antimicrobial, which helps to prevent moulds forming, it can be a solvent to extract nutrients, and it can also act as a medium for easier absorption of those nutrients. Herbs for medicinal purposes have long been preserved in alcohol (as well as dehydrated, infused, fermented, set in vinegar and so on). Alcohol is a powerful way to preserve. I love to think about the benefits of herbs when I'm making a drink, but please be aware that, when fermented, some can indeed be potent. Remember that these recipes aren't designed to be consumed in large amounts.

Functional or healthy alcohol seems a bit of a sales pitch, an oxymoron to most, but I am referring to the very low amounts found in kombucha and water kefir, for example, sitting between .5 to 3% ABV (alcohol by volume). As previously discussed, many of the wild yeasts we are relying on to ferment the drinks in this book don't tolerate a high alcohol content. As the alcohol level rises, the yeasts that make the alcohol die off. If you'd like a higher alcohol content you will probably need to add yeasts grown specifically for that purpose. But this book is more about traditional, spontaneous fermentation and the alcohol is more of a by-product. The liqueurs in this book, on the other hand, are very strong and are designed for sipping in small quantities when enjoyed as a bitter or digestive.

However, I think it's important to know about your brew and so I urge you to get comfortable with using a hydrometer or refractometer. Not for the kombucha and kefir type drinks, but the wines, beers and meads. Both tools are fairly easy to use - follow the instructions they come with. Measure the sugars before you ferment and the remaining sugars after the brew is done, and then do the calculation; it's a simple minus and multiplication. Keep a notebook or fermenting diary and record your brew's sugar levels for future reference. It will be invaluable so you can look back on each brew and learn from the process, blends and ratios used. Note that it is too late to measure the percentage of alcohol in your drink after it is made without specialist equipment.

Just be aware that these testing methods are good for the more common home brews like beer and wine, but not entirely accurate for the living brews like kombucha, jun and water kefir. These differ because they contain other residual solids (cellulose, yeast, bacteria), so the reading will show a slightly higher alcohol measure than it actually is. If you need a more accurate measure, you can take your brews to a laboratory, but make sure they understand the nature of your brew and measure with gas chromatography, for example.

OTHER KITCHEN BITS AND PIECES

CLOTH

Always have cotton fabric and muslin (cheesecloth) in your home to use at will for your ferments. Cut and use squares of clean cloth for straining, draining, containing or simply loosely covering a ferment jar. Brew shops have good cotton bags that are great for steaming rice in. You might be able to source the kind of synthetic cloth that rice won't stick to when cooking from a good Asian food store. A nice clean pillow slip or cotton bag will also work wonders. Tea towels, and other fine but porous fabrics also work well. Just think about the weave and what size particles you're trying to keep out.

BREW OR SPARGE BAG

You won't see that awful word anywhere else in the book but you'll see it in brewing shops and books. It is both a noun and a verb – to sparge (wash and strain) and to use a sparge bag. It is really just a very large cloth tea bag designed to hold your grains or fruit, to keep the particles separate from your brew, that is easy to pull out, strain and squeeze etc. You can buy specialised brew/sparge bags or make your own. You can also find various sizes of unbleached cotton bags for hops and herbs and tea online. Or just use some cotton or muslin (cheesecloth) and tie it together to make a rough bag.

JUICER

This is a wonderful tool for the home kitchen but also for fermentation. There are various types and models on the market. Look for one that juices fibrous things like ginger well. I've had a masticating juicer for more than twenty years now. It has a chewing and grinding action and can make nut butters and turn frozen fruit into an ice cream consistency. I also use the 'grass' juicer and grain mill attachments.

STEAMERS

I use the bamboo stacking steamers not just for steaming but to ferment things that need a bit of airflow while being covered, put away – even stacked – such as hairy tofu and cheeses. I also use them to steam rice for kōji and then later for drying the kōji out. Once you scale up, go ahead and upgrade to a larger metal system stacker. I was loyal to the bamboo one and took way too long to upgrade. Never looked back. A steam oven and warming drawer? Lucky you.

JUGS, BOWLS AND BUCKETS

You'll need multiple non-reactive bowls and pots, but nothing out of the ordinary. It makes life easier to have a bowl with a lip or spout for pouring, and a few different sizes of jugs. People don't usually have a large 5 litre (170 fl oz) jug, but I love mine. I prefer glass or stainless steel; ceramic is great too but heavy. Food-grade plastic tubs and buckets are easy to find and can be good for storage as well as for using as a fermenting vessel.

STRAINERS

Have a few sizes that can sit on bowls, buckets, cups and in funnels. Sometimes, you'll need very fine mesh, other times – as with milk kefir – you'll need it to be a bit more open. There are high-end paper filters that cocktail makers

FERMENTATION ACCOUTREMENTS: SIPHON, STRAINER, GLASS VESSELS, FUNNEL, SPARGE BAG, AIRLOCK, MORTAR AND PESTLE, MUSLIN, AND TWINE

and coffee brewers use. They work well for clarification; otherwise, a small piece of cloth to line your sieve to catch any tiny bits works well.

FUNNELS
It's good to have a few different funnels, including for larger jars and narrow neck bottles. My very favourite funnel also has an integrated strainer. So handy.

STIRRERS AND SPOONS
I love a long stick for stirring my various brews. They have become a fun thing to find on a walk and bring home. I then sit and peel the bark off and whittle and shape the stick slightly. I have one just for milk kefir, one for mead and beers and one for wild sodas. Dry the wood after stirring – the yeasts just might stay on, dormant and waiting to repopulate your next brew. Of course, a long handled wooden, stainless steel or plastic spoon is designed for this and you can buy the really long ones at your local home brew store.

BOTTLES AND BOTTLING

Unless you are making large volumes of drinks, you'll only need strainers, a funnel, jugs, jars and sealable bottles for the bottling process. It might be worth buying or borrowing a siphon tube or an auto siphon kit and bottling gun if you start increasing production of beer or wine, and even more so if you really want to avoid the sediment and are serious about introducing less oxygen when transferring between vessels.

Collect a variety of jars and bottles with lids, so you have the sizes you need for the drinks you're making: some small ones for your liqueurs, large 5 litre (170 fl oz) jars and glass bottles in useful sizes (usually 330, 450, 500 or 750 ml/11–25½ fl oz). Not having enough bottles or the right sizes is a tedious oversight which can lead to people delaying bottling and ending up overfermenting their drinks. Be organised: save and source lots of bottles so this doesn't happen.

Thick, good quality, undamaged glass bottles are best. Those with flip-top lids are great; they seal the bottle so it can carbonate and you can flip the lid off when the pressure builds. They can be a bit pricey if you're buying a lot of them, so it's probably a good idea to source some cheaper ones too. If you are collecting used glass bottles, just make sure the seals and lids are intact. To re-use bottles with a crown seal (like most beer bottles), you'll need a supply of new lids and a clamping tool which can all be found online or at your local home brewery store. As with fermentation vessels, don't get caught buying cheap, colourful bottles with lots of curves and corners and handles – bends and joins are weak spots and they often can't take the pressure and explode.

New or recycled plastic bottles are a bit of a last resort but will certainly reduce any blowouts and breakages. They also make it super easy to see if the brew is ready by the bulge in the bottle.

SIPHONING OR RACKING

The process of siphoning is the transfer of your ferment using suction, gravity and tubing to avoid catching the yeasts and lees that sit at the bottom of your brew. Siphoning out to avoid mixing the sediment in is called racking.

One vital and free resource in siphoning and bottling is gravity. Raise your fermenting vessel up quite a bit higher than your bottles – using books or bricks or a kitchen bench with the bottles on the ground, for example – and use the tube to siphon and bottle.

There are lots of types of siphoning gear, from just a simple clear tube with which to create a suction vacuum, to fancier auto siphon types with sediment blockers. Using tubes is also good to minimise the liquid's contact with the air when you're bottling. Note that siphoning gear will need sanitising before each use, as with all equipment (see page 20).

To work a siphon

Your siphon should come with directions, but if you haven't used one before, it's easy. For the pumping method, place the siphon or bottling wand into your brew and draw the liquid out with the pump that comes with the siphon. Alternatively, you can place the tubing into a bowl of sanitised water to fill it up and create a vacuum, or you can use suction to draw the liquid from the source vessel through the hose. In all cases, ensure one end of the hose is placed in your brew, make sure any remaining air is pushed out through the other end of the tube, then guide the hose to the containers to be filled (below the level of the liquid in the source vessel) and start siphoning. As soon as the hose starts siphoning, the liquid will come rushing out, so be ready to stop it with your thumb or a clamp and attach a bottle gun to the end if you are using one. Remember to position the brew higher than the bottling vessels by placing it on a chair, bench or another bucket, for example.

Brew

BREW

DRINK YOUR GRAINS

Grains – unlike fruit and vegetables – need a certain kind of coaxing before the yeasts can enjoy their bounty. Life is certainly easier for yeasts that feed on grapes to make wine, or apples for cider, as the sugar is just under the skin. Grains contain plenty of sugar, but it is in the form of starch – this is the reason we need an extra step here and there.

The following are beers and brews for your kitchen, not a shed. They are small enough to sit and ferment in a jar or a pot on your kitchen bench – or tucked away somewhere – and can be made with tools you already have. No need to move outside and buy pulleys and tanks.

Grain fermentation has more variables than the other ferments in this book, so I recommend you start small. Brewing in smaller amounts allows you to be more creative as there is less at stake: no-one wants to lose twenty litres, but four isn't as painful, right? I'm not saying you'll fail with the following recipes, but brewing small means there is less pressure, less risk and less storage. More fun and more flavour options. This is very much a less is more situation.

MAKING MAKGEOLLI

Broomsticks
and Sugidama

Around the world, and over time, we have had many ways of letting people know a brew was ready: putting something out front or making a noise or walking the streets and singing to sell the brews.

Long ago, but not *that* long ago, when a batch of beer was made and ready to sell, a broom would be placed at the front door and all passers-by would know there was a fresh batch of beer for sale. During the brew, this bunch of porous branches, often birch, would sit in the bottom of the beer, soaking up yeasts. When the brew was ready, they were easily pulled out as they were attached to a pole – like a broomstick. The brewstick was placed outside – branches forward – to dry. These branches were important as they hosted the yeasts: the magic required to make the next brew, to inoculate it.

In that pre-preservative era, fresh beer was all there was. The beer was nourishing, alive, a source of food, and it was most often women who brewed it, just as they baked the bread; they carried flavour and life on their hands. They brewed in large pots or cauldrons, over a flame, sometimes with grains, often without, adding ingredients such as mugwort and wormwood, nettles and spruce, and other seasonal flavours that made their drinkers feel good. The water would be sanitised by the boil and safe to drink. We were yet to learn about the tiny unseen microbial world; instead, there was an air of mystery, a trust in magic attached to brewing. Beer was often safer than water to drink.

Beer and bread require plenty of grain, so these small family brewhouses had plenty of cats to keep the mice away. The female brewsters wore tall hats so that, as they walked the streets selling their wares, their customers could spot them easily to buy and enjoy a fresh pot on the spot. A broomstick, some cats, a pointy hat and a cauldron. Stirring and adding herbs to a brew on a fire.

When it was found (by Hildegard von Bingen) that hops preserved beer and gave it a recognisable bitter flavour, momentum grew: beer could now be scaled up and sold to be transported to other towns. A profitable commodity.

Monks, already following a principle of self-sufficiency, had made it their duty to provide drinks and food to travellers and were allowed the time to learn deeply and record their work, exchange knowledge and improve upon it. They had land and well-tended apothecary gardens, and by the fifth century, over 600 monasteries were brewing beer and offering it to adults and children, even enjoying their brews during fasting.

Before long, the brews made and sold at home were touted as inferior and unfavourable, the brewsters vilified, their brews too mysterious, seen as dirty, the brewer portrayed as ugly and their beer as suspicious – perhaps with a spell on it, or even poisonous. The female home brewers began to be made out as untrustworthy, as witches, and their beer something to be avoided. There was now a safer, more commercial option – taxable and therefore also encouraged and supported by people in power.

So it didn't take long before the beer left the hands of women, their income no longer as readily supplemented nor supported by their village. It was perhaps a beginning of our current problem in food and drink where quantity – scalability – mattered more than quality. The commercial beer widely available now is made on a super large scale (even the smaller brewers) and is quite different from beer's beginnings: the alcohol is higher, the fizz is added, and it's certainly no longer seen as a food source. Nor is it really that good for you.

In the Basque country of Spain, where apple cider is embedded in the culture, a wooden instrument called a txalaparta, made from the same boards that pressed the cider apples, is clapped together to summon the neighbours – to let them know that their collective efforts have paid off and it is time to come together and enjoy the brew. A celebration ensues, with the txalaparta played like an instrument while the cider is enjoyed and traditional dances are performed. The drink, sagardoa, has never really changed – unlike beer – nor did religion take it over. It hasn't been made more alcoholic, and for the most part there aren't that many breweries that mass-produce it. That said, it's very hard to find a good version of this raw apple cider outside of Basque country. Extended families still pick apples from shared plots and get together every year to make the cider and later divvy up the brew. Because it is low in alcohol, it's also readily enjoyed at home with meals, as it has been throughout time.

At about the time that beer, ciders and wines were first crafted in Europe and Africa, people in Asia, Australia and North and South America were also fermenting with saps, sugars from fruits and vegetables, and grains and fungi. These would eventually become the varieties of rice-based brews, beers and toddies we know well today. In Japan, cedar leaves were made into a giant ball called a sugidama. It was strung outside of a brewhouse to let customers know the age of the brew inside. Over time, the foliage would turn from green to brown; when it was brown, the sake was ready.

In a familiar trajectory, sake became more technical when it was mostly taken out of the hands of small family brewers, and shrines and temples were made guardians of the brew. This was later followed by larger specialist breweries that grew kōji specific to sake brewing. This art became easy to transport and taxable. Like elsewhere, the recipes and technique of brewing that were formerly the domain of the home or cottage industry were now owned and no longer shared as recipes should be. Laws were formed around how to brew, where and by

whom. Money ruled this industry much earlier than it did the food industry. I think we have diminished our knowledge (and our power) in what appears to be a bid for an easier life. Luckily, the revival in doing things and making things ourselves from scratch is strong – and you are part of it by reading and using this book. Recipes are for sharing.

It has been said that humans began to settle because of our love of grains and fermenting them for these drinks. Many cultures stopped being entirely nomadic not just because they needed to grow grains en masse, but because of the time it took to ferment and the need for vessels and other accoutrements. The collective human relationship with naturally fermented drinks is ancient, neolithic even. We have found ways to work with nature to convert sugars into flavourful, fermented, lightly alcoholic and usually effervescent drinks. This can be through plants and fruit, or from starch within a grain, with honey or sap from trees, or from moulds both visible and microscopic, on and in and all around us. The yeast on our hands, like those invited to live in the birch branches, can start a brew. Even the enzyme in our saliva was – and in places still is – used to convert starchy grains to glucose. From Japan to Africa, there are methods that involve chewing grain and spitting it into the brew to start the fermentation process. Early on, we somehow worked out that germinating (or malting) a grain activates an enzyme (diastase) that, similar to our spit, also converts the starch in the grain to sugar. Stories abound of people discovering many of these techniques by accident, followed by trial and error. Plant life, fungi and bacteria – no matter the ingredients, or the way they interact – give us amazing, often sparking and stimulating drinks, different yet of the same vein, no matter where we are in the world.

And here we are now – you're here with me. And we are going back to small scale, celebrating 'batch variance' with smaller

benchtop amounts, in our kitchens, made by families or friends, together or alone – to reap the rewards of your garden, save a season, to create something unique, maybe even to bring a bit more money in.

Humans seem to be always moving – trying to get somewhere better, ahead, to the next level, aiming for progress. Fermenting makes you look forward while keeping you rooted: working with things from the earth that you can't create – water, soil, fungi and the microbial world. The beauty of wild drinks is perhaps that we need to look back and re-learn in order to move forward.

RYE BREAD KVASS

This beautiful kvass is the most delicious way there is to use old bread. Depending on your bread and the other ingredients you add, such as herbs, spices, honey or sugar, you'll get a frothy, impressive brew that tastes like a cross between apple cider and beer. This brew is refreshing and good on its own but excellent in a cocktail: we've mixed it with smoky whiskeys and bourbons and have deliberately smoked the bread a bit extra, outside over a fire, to intensify the flavour.

Kvass is a traditional Russian and Eastern European ferment. In some places, you can still buy it on street corners from mobile vendors who will fill bottles and pots on the spot. Like beer, kvass was once a staple for farmers: a nutritious food source and energy enhancer, a tonic and a thirst-quenching drink all in one. It also makes good use of stale bread, which you can collect in the freezer until you have enough.

The first time we made a large vat of this I was willingly setting us up for a public failure. Alla Wolf-Tasker, our local mentor, hotelier and food doyenne, had invited a famous Russian chef to Daylesford, Australia, for a ticketed dinner. They decided to pair a rye kvass with one of the dishes and she called to see if I could make it. I boldly said yes, even though I'd never really made more than a couple of litres at a time for anyone but myself. To successfully brew and meet the standards of both a childhood memory (Alla) and a visiting, patriotic chef (the Russian) was really asking for trouble. We only had a week from when she called until the dinner. But it worked. Maybe not just like 'home' but delicious nonetheless.

BREW 43

RYE KVASS

Prep. 30 minutes | Ferment 5-10 days |
Equipment: 3-5 L (101-170 fl oz) jar, muslin (cheesecloth), bottles

To get in the swing of kvass, make this version first to wrap your
fermenting brain around working with bread as an ingredient in a drink.
This base flavour is my favourite anyway.

INGREDIENTS

400 g (14 oz) dark rye bread,
  cubed (see Note)
2 litres (68 fl oz/8 cups) water
125 g (4½ oz) organic raw sugar
50 g (1¾ oz) raw honey
75 g (2¾ oz) malt
1 tablespoon raisins (organic,
  no oil)
small piece of orange zest
1-2 sprigs of mint

Preheat the oven to 180°C (360°F), with the aim to slightly burn the bread.
I have had lovely results by toasting the bread over a fire or in a wood-fired
bread or pizza oven. The smoky flavour really translates well in the kvass.

Spread the cubed bread on a baking tray and roast until dried into rusks.
If you are after a deep smoky caramel flavour, turn the oven up and burn
the bread in parts. You want each piece to have dark to very dark patches
on them rather than completely blackened, so keep an eye on the tray.
Drying and then burning the bread is important as it brings the available
sugars to the surface.

Remove from the oven and cool.

Pour the water into the jar, add the sugar, honey and malt. Stir well.
Add the raisins, orange zest and mint and give it a vigorous stir. Lastly, add
the toasted bread. Cover the jar loosely with a cloth secured with a rubber
band and leave to sit on a bench to ferment, plunging the bread and stirring
gently daily. The bread will rise to the top – if you let it just sit on the surface
it will likely attract unwanted yeast growth, so pop it back into the liquid
frequently.

Taste after 5 days, and if it is souring nicely with a hint of fizz, it's ready.
It could take 7 days or more depending on the temperature in your room.
Be guided by flavour: is it excitingly sour, with a bit of sweetness and rich
flavour? Slightly effervescent? When those elements are present, strain the
solids out. If clarity is important to you, then strain again with a lined sieve
before transferring to bottles. If you think it needs more sugar, a little boost

to get fizzier, add a few extra raisins into each bottle at this second ferment stage. As a general rule, if a ferment is not that fizzy and has no sweetness or sugars left to offer, adding dried fruit like raisins will feed the yeasts and kickstart the carbonation.

Lid the bottles and sit them out for a further 24 hours before refrigerating. You'll notice a layer of sediment resting at the bottom, particularly if you didn't strain a second time. When you drink any wild ferments like this, you can choose to either gently swirl the sediment into the brew or pour carefully to keep the sediment at the bottom depending on how you like it. Don't shake it – it will become super fizzy and hard to pour.

Kvass is served chilled. Once opened, consume within a day or two. It may froth somewhat on top; you can just scoop it off if it bothers you, or stir it into the brew.

NOTES: Cube and freeze stale bread leftovers until you have enough. If you make sourdough at home and have a sourdough mother, you might like to add a tablespoon of it with the bread.

VARIATIONS

Have a play with these variations on the base kvass recipe (page 44), using a kind of bread and a natural, fermentable sugar to feed the yeasts.

HOT CROSS BUN OR RAISIN TOAST KVASS

Replace the rye bread with hot cross buns (or a dense raisin bread).

Add a cinnamon stick, 2 cloves, 5 cardamom pods and a few strips of orange zest. Add a tablespoon of extra raisins, stir and taste. Omit the mint.

RHUBARB AND COFFEE KVASS

You might call this a breakfast kvass.

Keep the rye bread or swap out with any plain sourdough bread.

In a saucepan, cook 200 g (7 oz) chopped rhubarb with a splash of brewed coffee until tender. You may need to add more coffee as it softens. Cool and add to your jar, top with 100 g (3½ oz) roasted whole coffee beans, 1 cinnamon stick, 2–5 allspice berries and a split vanilla pod. Leave the orange zest in if you like, but omit the mint. Add the toasted bread and water. Remember to stir every day.

CACAO AND BLACK PEPPER KVASS

Replace the malt with honey (120 g/4½ oz). If you're thinking ahead, infuse the honey: add 2 stems of culinary lavender to the honey and ferment together (see page 107).

Steep 30 g (¼ cup) cracked cacao nibs and 1 tablespoon black pepper in 250 ml (8½ fl oz/1 cup) boiled water for 10 minutes and add to your fermenting jar. If you're not using infused honey, add 1–2 lavender flowers and the honey to the jar. If the season is right, 5 strawberries or other sweet berries go well in this too. Omit the orange and mint. Rye bread works best here. Pop in the bread and sugar, raisins and water. Cover and leave to ferment, making sure to stir and check the brew.

APRICOT RYE KVASS

Add ½ cup chopped dried apricots or 1 cup fresh (about 6 medium) apricots. I also add 1 tablespoon caraway seeds (adjust depending on your preference). Omit the orange and mint or just add a smaller amount. If you want more apricot flavour at the end, you could pop 1–2 extra apricots into each bottle for a second ferment.

KITCHEN BENCH BEER

Take grains, heat, yeast and water and you have beer. It was a revelation to me that I could make a hop-free beer in my kitchen in a large jar, just like other fermented drinks. More than the other ferments, this is what sent me down a path of sourcing, growing and foraging things such as mugwort and wormwood.

Simplified, malt is just grain that has sprouted and then been roasted. It is an important part of the billion-dollar highly industrialised beer industry. On a small scale, malt is easily made at home, in your kitchen (see page 56). I was already sprouting grains for other drinks, so I was halfway to malt without knowing it. I just had to add the roasting stage. That said, I suggest that for your first brews, you buy malt for beer. Once you're familiar and happy with the process, malting your own grain in small batches will make a cool 'from scratch and locally sourced' addition to your brews.

SPROUTING GRAINS

SPROUTING GRAINS

Soaking and sprouting a grain, legume or nut will bring it to life – it is germination. Sprouted grains and seeds add value to any meal or ferment, and sprouting is a very straightforward, predictable process. It will also make the grains or legumes more delicious and more digestible, eliminate the phytic acid and increase bionutrients.

Grains are dormant. When you put them in water, they wake up, and life in the form of a little sprout appears. Sprouting grains for consumption – not just in fermentation – enhances the grain and makes it easier to transform (as we do when we brew). Soaking is used to activate a grain, to make it easier to cook, or to break down the complex sugars.

Sprouting is a cycle of washing, soaking, draining and rinsing grains, and giving them time in the right growing conditions for sprouts to form. If you add a longer drying-out stage, or variations of a roasting stage, then you are malting (page 56).

Equipment

You can use almost any tray or container you have at home, but there are many purpose-built designs available. Lid kits with strainers or screens that will fit onto wide-mouth jars (which you may already have for fermenting) are a good purchase, as are layered sprouting trays. If you are using different grains, I recommend using a separate jar or tray for each as they tend to germinate differently.

You can make your own complete system with a jar, covered with a square of netting, screen or cloth secured with an elastic band. I have had great success using a seed tray, lining it with a damp paper towel and spreading the grains out so they are about 20 mm (½ in) high and just deep enough to generate some warmth. Sit them somewhere warm and sunny.

How to

Wash the grains, cover with water and let them soak in a bowl or jar overnight.

Drain the water, rinse the grains again and shake out any excess water. Let the grains sit in your sprouting vessel. Repeat the rinsing, vigorous draining and sitting morning and evening – every 8–10 hours – until sprouting magic happens. Between rinses, keep the sprouting jar tilted to aid drainage. If too wet, the grains will develop mould rather than wake up. When I use the tray method, I move the grains about with my hand and keep them covered with a tea towel that I sometimes spray with water to keep them damp.

You are looking for little tails – not every grain needs to have one, but most should. It should only take a couple of days and, just like fermenting, you'll have something coming to life right there in your kitchen.

TIP: If you keep chickens, you'll only need to use half as much seed for their feed if you sprout it. This will save you money and make the chickens happy as it is good for their little guts, too.

BREWING BASICS

Sugar is important in fermentation. It is readily available in fruit; however, in grains, sugar comes in the form of starch that needs to be converted into more easily fermentable sugars. Soaking or sprouting the grain makes it easier to break down. Enzymes then do the critical work of making sugars available for yeasts. After that there are six key stages:

1. Malt In beer making, the sprouted grain is malted: dried, toasted or roasted, and cracked. You can think of malt as both a process and an ingredient.

2. Mash or steep Grains are steeped in hot water to make the sugars easier to release. In beer, the brewing water becomes the drink. Usually, when you cook a grain, you keep the grain and toss the water, right? In beer the wort (say 'wert' – the liquid drawn from the strained grains) is kept and the grains are the by-product. If you're being creative, this is the stage where you might add another source of sugar – something starchy with flavour, such as sweet potatoes. The sweet liquid is the base of your beer (makgeolli and sake, pages 58 and 66, differ in that the malts and the steeping liquid are left to ferment together and strained later).

3. Sparge Sparging is straining and rinsing the grain mash over the wort to make sure all the sugars are extracted. With rice beers, you'd press the grains at this point.

4. Boil and cool Cook the wort and maybe add hops, other greens and any spices. This is where you get your cauldron on and stir and bubble and boil. We are making flavours here.

5. Ferment Now add the yeast, stir, shut it into your brew vessel and let it sit. You've almost done all you can. Within about 6 hours, you may see some action. Wait.

6. Bottle Lid and rest your brew to get more carbonation. Sometimes this needs help, and a form of sugar is added.

NOTE: There is a lot of grain leftover from all the brews in this chapter. Using the spent grain in a home kitchen is more manageable when you brew in small batches as we are. See pages 212–3 for some ideas on uses.

BEER IN A JAR

This beer recipe requires equipment you'll commonly have in your kitchen already and only a few things you may need to source. It is a great starting point; with time you might start to grow your own yeast, or perhaps malt your own grains, and if you don't already, possibly grow your own hops and herbs.

First we cook, then we strain and ferment. Beer brewing techniques and types come with a lot of jargon which is a bit of a turn off because it makes it seem more difficult than it is. Wort, mash out, lauter, sparge, adjuncts, attenuation, vorlauf – it's a long list. I won't use many of those terms here.

CARROT SEED ALE

Prep. 3½ hours | Fermentation time: up to 14 days |
Equipment: 2 × 5 L (170 fl oz) jars (see Notes), thermometer, muslin (cheesecloth), siphon with tubing, bottles

Carrot seed is used in many traditional drinks and tonics. Carrots are in the same family as caraway, asafoetida, dill, anise, fennel and cumin and they all tend to be very good for digestion and therefore gut health.

INGREDIENTS

5 litres (170 fl oz) water
1 kg (2 lb 3 oz) crushed malt
  (see Notes)
100 g (3½ oz) carrots, washed and
  chopped
500 g (1 lb 2 oz) spray malt
  (powdered malt)
50 g (1¾ oz) carrot seeds (see
  Notes), in a small muslin bag
15 g (½ oz) dry hops (see Notes)
2.5 g (½ teaspoon) brewer's yeast
  (Saison or American ale)

Priming sugar
30 g (2 tablespoons) brown sugar
100 ml (3½ fl oz) warm water

Heat the water to 70°C (158°F) in a large saucepan. Add the crushed malt and carrots, stirring every 15 minutes for 1 hour, aiming to keep the mash at around 70°C (158°F). Right before you take it off the heat, increase to

80°C (175°F). This little increase in heat is important as it will stop any more enzymatic action happening and lock the flavour in. Take off the heat.

Line a strainer with muslin, place over a large bowl and strain out the malt and carrots, leaving them in the strainer.

Pour the liquid into a large jug to measure what you have. Some of the water will have evaporated. Top it up to 4.5 litres (152 fl oz) if it has reduced, then return the liquid – your wort – to the saucepan, heating until it reaches 70°C (158°F).

Return the strainer, still with the malt and carrots, to a large bowl or another pot. Pour the hot liquid over the malt and into the bowl. Put the strainer on the other pot or bowl and pour the liquid over this. Repeat this straining over the solids between the bowls – pouring the liquid over the grains back and forth – 2 or 3 times, aiming to get as much sugar from the grain as possible and any particles out. The liquid should run clearer after this. Keep the spent grain if you plan to repurpose it (see pages 212–3).

Return the wort to the saucepan, bring to a boil over a high heat, then slowly add the spray malt and carrot seeds and stir gently. Lower the heat and simmer for 1 hour, adding hops toward the end, reserving a small amount to add at a later stage.

Cool the wort to 20°C (68°F) – you can speed this up by putting your pan into a sink of ice. While the wort is cooling, ready your strainer, funnel and fermenting vessel. There is no more heating after this, so everything really does need to be sanitised from here.

Strain and pour the wort into your fermenter – a jar or carboy. Use a funnel lined with cloth or another filter to catch the seed bag and hops. Make sure the jar isn't too full – you need headroom of at least 2 cm (¾ in) for movement – but do check you still have 4.5 litres (152 fl oz). Top up with water if necessary. The correct volume becomes important for adding priming sugar later.

Add the yeast – we want the temperature to be warm enough to activate the yeast but not so hot that it kills it, so do this while the wort is still relatively warm. You also don't want the environment too cold or the yeast will remain dormant.

Stir and agitate vigorously or put the lid on the fermenter and shake and swirl it for about a minute to blend the yeast in and wake it up. Take the lid off and put the stopper and airlock on.

Aim to keep your beer at around 15–21°C (59–70°F). You may need to troubleshoot to find that sweet spot if your kitchen is very cold or very hot. A heating mat, sleeping bag, hot water bottles or electric blanket can help with this (see pages 24–5).

After about 3 days, your brew should start bubbling like crazy; this is a good reason to keep it in a place where hearing the bubbles will please you. After 14 days the bubbling will have settled somewhat, and it is time to bottle your brew. Do not try to bottle it early as it can overcarbonate in the bottle. Wait until your beer is not bubbling and the top of the brew is flat. If you can see bubbles going, wait a bit longer.

For the priming sugar, combine the sugar and water in a small pan over heat and stir until dissolved. This amount of sugar is designed for 4.5 litres (152 fl oz); too much sugar to liquid now would result in overcarbonation of your beer.

Pour the sugar liquid into a second 5 L (170 fl oz) pot, then siphon (or rack, see pages 32–3) the beer into the vessel to combine with the sugar syrup. Mix well. Alternatively, distribute the syrup evenly with a syringe into each individual bottle, then rack the beer into the bottles. You want to get the beer out without disturbing the yeast at the bottom.

When bottling, have your flip-top or crown seal lids and bottles sanitised. Set it up so the vessel you used for fermenting the beer is much higher than the bottles you are putting the beer into. Make sure the distance from the brew to the bottle is as far as possible for optimum flow. Stop racking just before you hit the sediment.

Make sure not to fill the bottles right to the top; leave a gap just like you see in store-bought bottled drinks. Lid with whatever system you have and sit the bottles out for a further 14 days.

Refrigerate and enjoy.

NOTES: I'd ferment this in a 5 L (170 fl oz) glass carboy with airlock and stopper, or in a fermenting jar.

Substitute carrot seed with caraway, celery or cumin seed, or a mixture, if you like.

If you are making your own malt for this, a blend of wheat and barley lightly toasted would suit this beer. I like to use a grassy or citrusy variety of hops, such as Cascade. Hops are sold in whole, plug or pelletised form.

MALTING

Malting is an artform in itself – like coffee roasting and blending. There used to be as many artisan malthouses as there were breweries, and both were located close to where the grains grew. With more and more farmers growing heritage grains today and craft brewers using them, small-batch malthouses are making a comeback (including perhaps in your kitchen).

Choose your grain: barley is great and reliable, but sorghum and wheat work well too. Your choice of grain and how you roast it will determine what flavours you end up with, so have a plan for what kind of beer you're making before you start. Do you want a caramelly burnt smoky flavour? Or toasty? Choose your grain and roast accordingly.

First, sprout your chosen grains (see pages 49-50). Allow up to 3 days for this step. You don't need any special equipment, I have used seed trays lined with damp cotton cloth lately, and as my confidence increases so does the amount I prepare. When the tails appear on the grains, it's time to roast.

Roasting grain for malt

Preheat your oven to 50°C (122°F). Spread the grain out on a baking tray and, for a light roast, roast for 2 hours. For a darker roast, increase the temperature to 75°C (167°F) for the second hour. Be sure that the oven temperature doesn't go higher than 80°C (176°F), otherwise the enzymes (which convert starch to sugar) that have formed in the sprouting (germination) process will be killed.

Malting enhances nutritional content of the grain and liquid malt extract has been used medicinally, often for people with digestive disorders. Diastase, the enzyme created in the malting stage, helps digestion of starchy foods whether in a fermenter, a glass bowl, or in the stomach.

NOTE: You can dry the sprouted grains first in a low oven or dehydrator and store in an airtight container for later use.

MUGWORT AND LEMON BEER

Prep. 1 hour | Fermentation time: 10 days |
Equipment: 4 L (135 fl oz) jar with airlock, thermometer, siphon
with tubing, bottles

Before hops became popular, all manner of available herbs were used for bittering and flavouring beers. Mugwort was one of them. A beer without hops is known as a gruit ale. We don't hear much of mugwort in a lot of Western cooking, but it has been a common ingredient in the past and remains so in some places to this day. All over Europe, Africa and Asia, mugwort has been eaten, smoked, steeped, cooked and applied externally. It is considered a protector from disease, a medicine and a dream enhancer. You may have to grow your own to get a decent supply as it is hard to come by in regular greengrocers.

INGREDIENTS

3.5 litres (118 fl oz) water
about 15–20 dried mugwort leaves
550 g (1 lb 3 oz) brown sugar
  (see Note), plus extra for
  priming
3 large lemons, juiced
5 g (1 teaspoon) brewer's yeast
  (Fermentis S-04 or US-05) or
  250 ml (8½ fl oz/1 cup) ginger
  beer mother (see page 130)
handful of juniper berries

Mix the water, mugwort and brown sugar in a large saucepan. Add the lemon juice and boil for 30 minutes. Cool the mixture down as quickly as possible to about 21°C (70°F). Once cooled, add your yeast source.

Strain and pour into your fermenter, add the juniper berries, then seal with an airlock lid. Let brew for 10 days.

Siphon into bottles (see pages 32–3), adding a ½ teaspoon of brown sugar to each bottle to assist in carbonation. Lid the bottles and let ferment for a few weeks. Keep an eye on them.

NOTES: Sugar could be replaced by fruit, concentrated sweetener such as the date syrup on page 179 or honey, or a mixture of all. You can use wild yeast starter from water kefir or yeast from another beer.

MAKGEOLLI – KOREAN RICE BEER

When I lived in Tokyo in my twenties, there was an alleyway strip we would visit late at night. We'd sit on cushioned milk crates around makeshift tables that balanced small tabletop grills. We ordered bites of food to cook ourselves, the night behind us, faces lit up over the flame. These meals were some of the cheapest, most memorable and delicious ever. The makgeolli (say ma*hk*-oli) was poured from a metal teapot and we drank from matching cups that were more like shallow bowls.

Let's talk about makgeolli. In Korean language, makgeolli can be translated as 'roughly strained', and the drink does have a murky liquor beneath a golden clear liquid layer. This beautiful lively drink is an enzyme-rich, slightly fizzy, delicious and milky-looking brew made from rice fermented with wheat and other grains. Its alcohol level ranges from 6–17%, which gives it the reputation for being a communal, happy drink, and nutritious enough to have been a staple among physical labourers. Makgeolli has made a comeback. It can be found in restaurants, bars, and vending machines in Korea and, more recently, also in the West. Many of the drinks on offer are not a good representation of the real thing, but they are a start. For a better result, learn to make it yourself.

In Korea, people drink makgeolli with their lunch even in aged care – it's a pick-me-up, full of digestive enzymes, and it also relaxes and calms. Do you need another reason? Makgeolli is said to have at least ten times more *Lactobacillus* than yoghurt; it is rich in protein, has seven essential amino acids, inositol and choline, fibre and vitamins B and C. (It is still an alcoholic drink, so obviously the health benefits should be framed within that context).

While makgeolli doesn't actually *spoil* thanks to the bacteria and yeast, its effervescence will increase over time and the flavour changes as well. Makgeolli that is lower in alcohol doesn't have a long shelf life and needs to be kept refrigerated. It is at its best for a fortnight, then slowly becomes less enjoyable over a few months, before taking on a new flavour profile after about 5 months.

Nuruk is to makgeolli what bread is to kvass, malt is to beer and kōji is to sake. The first few times you make makgeolli, just go out and buy the nuruk at a Korean or Asian food store; you'll likely find packets of this fermentation starter with the word 'enzymes' on it. If you are into it on a deeper level, as many fermenters are, make nuruk yourself (pages 63–5).

BASIC MAKGEOLLI RECIPE

Prep. 30 minutes | Fermentation time: 7 days-3 weeks |
Equipment: 2-5 L (68-170 fl oz) fermenting jar, muslin
(cheesecloth), bottles

INGREDIENTS

    1 kg (2 lb 3 oz) glutinous rice
      (sweet rice or Chapsaal, see
      Notes)
    100 g (2½ oz) nuruk (see page 63;
      cake or powdered)
    1 litre (34 fl oz/4 cups) water

The preparation of the rice is important. Wash, soak, drain and dry the rice
well, then steam it (see pages 75–6 for details of all four steps). Cool the
rice by spreading it out thinly on several trays or racks.

In a large bowl, crumble the nuruk over the cooled rice, then pour over the
water. Massage the nuruk and rice with your (very clean) hands. This part
is important, so spend some time combining the rice grains and nuruk,
aerating the mixture and waking it up somewhat – it feels nice.

In Korean, the word 'son-mat' means 'flavour of the hand'. Figuratively,
it means the taste of food you've made: with love, with time, with effort,
with your hands. The resulting flavour is one that is unique to you and your
efforts. This is where you put your heart in. At this point in your makgeolli
blending, perhaps think about your own son-mat and relax into the process:
no rushing, just good vibes. The next time you see your brew it will have a
whole different life within it.

Transfer the mixture into your fermenting jar and wipe down the inside of
the jar with a very clean cloth to deter unwanted moulds. The texture at this
stage will seem like porridge, and perhaps a bit dry, but this will change
within a few days. Lid your vessel: an airlock is great, or just sit your lid
on top to allow any carbon dioxide to leave as it wishes. Wipe down the
outside of the fermenter, and label with the date and expected finish date.

Put your brew in a room at a temperature of 18–21°C (64–70°F). Make
sure to stir a couple of times a day for the first 2–3 days. You'll notice
it becoming more liquid after the first few days. Stirring is important for
oxygenation and making sure that a variety of yeasts are growing and
replicating well, and also to make sure no yeasts sit on top of your brew
and establish there. Leave the jar for 7 days to 3 weeks depending on the
room temperature.

How do you know how long to sit it for? The benefit of a glass fermenting
jar for beginners is that you can see what is going on in your vessel. Watch
your brew. You'll know it's ready when the bubbles are slowing and there

is a clear liquid separate from the rice mixture. Stir this together and check if the rice breaks down easily between your fingers. Taste the liquid too; it should be lively and not too sweet or sour.

Note that at this stage, you could rack the top liquid off for a more refined drink that was once distilled into soji. Enjoyed like this it is no longer makgeolli but cheongju. The lees still in the bottle can be used as a kind of starter – you can add water, plain or infused, or with some pieces of fruit, and then sit it back in the fridge to ferment a bit longer. This drink you make with the sediment is where makgeolli had its beginnings as a 'seconds' to the more refined brew.

When your makgeolli is ready for bottling, stir the mixture well and then gently and slowly pour it into a cloth-lined strainer. Squeeze or press your cloth down to get all the liquid out, but don't force the lees through too much. Pour the brew into clean bottles, lid and refrigerate. Sediment will sink to the bottom: either pour carefully to keep it clear, or tilt gently to blend before drinking your sparkling brew. It will last for about 4 months kept in the fridge like this.

NOTES: Glutinous rice will give you a sweeter brew, and regular table rice will give you a drier finish. You can use a combination of the two. If you are just starting out and are using glutinous rice, steaming the rice will give you the best results. There are other ways you can prepare the rice for makgeolli: grinding into a powder and making a paste, using the rice cooker method, drying the rice, making porridge and boiling the rice; each one will result in a different water content in the rice and will therefore influence the flavour.

Save the spent grain, called jigemi, for crackers (page 205) or other uses (see page 211).

As with all of your brews, I recommend you make some notes to refer back to. Document the date, weather, ingredients, things that happened and other observations so if a batch is particularly amazing you can do it again. If it's not quite right then you'll be able to examine why.

FLAVOURED MAKGEOLLI

After you've made a couple of batches of plain makgeolli you'll be confident to flavour it. It's a simple matter of substituting water for infused, flavoured water or blended fruit and water. When you are brewing with fruit, it is best to first freeze the fruit and then defrost it before adding to your brew to get the best flavour.

Berries, peaches, strawberries and persimmons work well, but so does a pumpkin spice flavour – seriously!

PEACH MAKGEOLLI

INGREDIENTS

```
1 kg (2 lb 3 oz) glutinous rice
120 g (4½ oz) nuruk (see opposite)
500 g (1 lb 2 oz) peach slices,
  frozen, thawed and blended
800 ml (27 fl oz) water
```

Follow the method for basic makgeolli (pages 60–1), adding the blended peaches with the water and combining with the rice as described. Because there is sugar in the fruit, expect this to be a livelier brew than the plain one.

NOTES: If flavouring with milder spices, teas, leaves such as mugwort, hops, dried flowers, roots (such as ginger), or starches (such as sweet potatoes), it is best to add them early to steam with the rice.

NURUK – MALT FOR MAKGEOLLI

Prep. 1 hour | Fermentation time: up to 14 days |
Equipment: large square of muslin (cheesecloth), circular form
(see Notes), cardboard box, newspaper, dried straw

Nuruk can come in various forms, but the most common is made of wheat. It is traditionally stamped into cakes, which are then placed in a warm room, turned and nurtured as you would a cheese. One variety is made out of ground rice and is usually shaped into a ball rather than a cake; it is then fermented on pine needles or dried mugwort. Others are a blend of grains, also shaped into balls. In the south of Korea, where it tends to be warmer, nuruk is formed into a puck-like disk, but as you go further north, the nuruk gets thicker and comes in a block.

Nuruk has been a part of Korean home brewing since the third century CE. Due to the different grains and the organic bedding material used, it can house several yeasts and bacteria (as opposed to the one mould found in kōji – *Aspergillus oryzae,* see page 74). Nuruk has *A. oryze,* but also *Rhizopus spp, Saccharomyces cerevisiae, Pichia anomala* and various strains of lactic acid bacteria. Naturally, this varies depending on the temperatures, location and materials used.

It is difficult to import the artisan types of nuruk. Unless you are in Korea, you won't see a large variety available to buy. One option is to make your own. You'll need to set aside a couple of weeks to make nuruk and get hold of some rice, wheat or oat straw (or dried mugwort) to wrap the shaped form in. This is a good project to do at the end of summer to store for when the weather is cooler and the environment more suitable for brewing.

INGREDIENTS

    1.5 kg (3 lb 5 oz) whole-wheat
      grain, or Job's tears (see
      page 86)
    300 ml (10 fl oz) water

Wash the grain thoroughly, then drain for at least 20 minutes, agitating the water out. The grain needs to be dry enough to grind.

Coarsely grind the wheat in a blender or mortar and pestle. You may need to do this in batches.

Place in a bowl. Sprinkle with the water, massaging as you go until the mixture holds together (test by forming a small ball, pressing tightly). Scrape onto the muslin and wrap tightly, like a present, ready to press into your chosen form. Wrap with intention, ready for some gentle pressure.

Set your form on top of cardboard or newspapers on the floor, and gently but forcibly squeeze the wrapped grain package into it.

You'll need to apply a lot of weight onto the nuruk parcel to get it compressed tightly. It's traditional to place it on the floor and stand on it with clean socked feet. If you have a tofu press, put the lid on and clamp the mix in. If using an open form or tin, place a piece of cardboard or a thin wad of newspapers on top as a kind of pad and apply pressure to it, pushing the nuruk into every corner of the form, expelling the air. The aim is to get the nuruk as flat and compact as possible.

When you have achieved that, take it to your workbench and remove the form. You should be able to unwrap the cloth and, all going well, the cake *should* remain together, without crumbling.

Line the cardboard box with the straw and lie the nuruk in it, completely encasing it with straw. Close the box tightly. Sit it somewhere warm, out of sunlight.

The first week is important for attracting mould spores. Keeping the temperature between 28–36°C (82–97°F) will attract the best mould for alcohol production. Keep the box tightly closed, only opening to turn the cake every 3 days. During the second week, keep the box slightly cracked open, maintaining the temperature, to allow mycelia to inoculate the middle of the cake while allowing moisture to evaporate. In the last week, the focus is mostly moisture removal, but we want the mould to fully penetrate. Keeping the box lid half open and raising the temperature by one or two degrees will help with any final evaporation. The most common nuruk failure is letting the cake dry out too quickly, thereby creating a hard shell that prevents the inner moisture from evaporating.

Once the nuruk is covered with white mould, it needs to cure in the sun. Sunlight is known to break down potentially harmful mycotoxins so this is an important step. The nuruk doesn't necessarily need to sit outside – a window with light streaming in will work. It should sit in the sun for a minimum of 12 hours, but keep an eye on it – it may take as long as a week to dry out completely.

Store your nuruk in a container or broken into a jar for when you are ready to make your next batch of makgeolli. Make sure to store nuruk in an airtight environment as humidity can cause it to degrade faster.

NURUK

NOTES: *The form is used to hold and shape the nuruk. Press the mixture into the form while it is still damp. You can use something like a sturdy cake tin, a tofu press, a cheese form or a robust box.*

As is common with inoculation methods, things don't always work out perfectly the first few times. This is normal for a beginner. Pay attention to the colour of the moulds – in nuruk production, bright yellow is the best! In Korean it is called 'gold enzyme' and it is the best for alcohol production. If the nuruk develops a black or pink mould you'll need to throw it out. So sad!

DOBUROKU (FARMHOUSE SAKE)

There is a lot of joy to be found in a glass of lightly effervescent homemade sake. The style of sake we are making here was traditionally brewed in Japan in family homes and farms, and enjoyed as a refreshing restorative drink – a tonic and source of nutrients for workers after a day on the farm. It was a rough and unrefined drop. If you strain the rice out, you'll have a cloudy, roughly filtered, raw (unpasteurised) sake (nama nigori). If you leave the rice in, you have a cloudy and robust drink known as doburoku.

Sake is sometimes referred to as a rice wine, but it has more in common with a beer. Where wine is a one-step process (fruit sugars feed the yeast to make alcohol) and beer is a two-step process (first get the sugars from the grain, then add the yeast to that sweet water), sake does it all at once – multiple parallel fermentation. The enzymes make the sugars available to the yeasts at the same time as the sugar is being transformed to alcohol. As we're using wild yeasts – which have a lower tolerance for alcohol – the sake you make at home won't have a high alcohol content, but it will still be an alcoholic drink.

You can make sake out of any kind of rice, but in Japan, specific rice strains are grown for it. The rice is then polished – sometimes abraded so far as to leave only a small core of rice – making the sugar-rich nucleus easier to reach. It's hard to get polished rice outside of Japan, but I think that it is unnecessary for the rough home-brew we are making. A good, organically grown, ideally rain-fed short-grain rice will do just fine. There are delicious sakes brewed using sprouted brown rice, too.

How you cook the rice will make a difference to the finished product: steaming over wood or coals is said to produce a better flavour. The water you use in sake also makes a difference – sake is 80% water – so use good, filtered water.

BODAIMOTO METHOD SAKE

Prep. 5-7 days for rice water | Fermentation time: 3-14 days |
Equipment: 3-5 L (101-170 fl oz) jar, cloth (or small hemp bags),
bottles (see Notes)

This is a wild sake. I first learned about it in Kyoto when I attended a residency program on growing kōji. This knowledge was reinforced by Masaru-san from Terada Honke sake brewery when he was our festival guest. I love the culture at their brewery, which has a generous spirit of sharing and encouraging the new and curious as well as enthusiasts. Happily, and gratefully, I have seen and felt this spirit of sharing and connecting with artisan traditions almost wherever I go. Most passionate people working with old traditions are eager to share what they know and hope that you can take something special from the experience.

The technique we are using here takes its lead from the Bodaimoto fermentation method developed by Shoraku Temple monks in Nara about six hundred years ago.

There is life and gut-loving digestive enzymes in your brew that you can feel inside you as you consume it, before also feeling the alcohol slowly warming your chest. No doubt you'll feel quite content with your work, which is another kind of warmth I like to encourage.

INGREDIENTS

600 g (1 lb 5 oz) rice, short-
  grain or koshihikari
700 ml (23½ fl oz) water
  (preferably rain or filtered)
100 g (3½ oz) cooked rice (see
  Notes)
350 g (1½ oz) prepared (dry) rice
  kōji (see Notes)

STEP 1: MAKE RICE WATER

This first step is aimed at creating a protective, lactic acid–rich water in which yeasts can grow without a lot of competition and become the dominant population. Because of the lactic acid, the water will slowly develop a distinctive sour smell that fermenters know well.

Wash and drain the rice well (follow the steps on pages 75–6; note: no soaking required in this recipe). Put the raw rice into the jar and add 700 ml (23½ fl oz) water.

RICE BALL ABOUT TO BE WRAPPED IN MUSLIN

Next, take the cooked rice and make it into two small balls, tying each ball up in a square of muslin (or use little hemp bags available for tea and herbal soups). Make sure each bag is securely closed, then add to the jar, fully submerging them in the water. If the balls are sitting too far above the water line, gently bury them down into the rice or flatten them out somewhat. You don't want any of the bag or rice balls exposed to the air, attracting moulds.

Cover the jar with a light cloth and secure it around the top with a rubber band. Leave the jar to sit somewhere where you can observe and access it easily. Every day, with a very clean hand, give the rice balls a squeeze, even a gentle massage. Say hello and send out love and good vibes as you do this. Push the bags gently back under the water and re-cover the jar.

Taste the water each time. It will slowly become sour, kind of lactic and reminiscent of yoghurt. The water will become cloudier and, within 2–4 days, depending on the temperature in your house, you might notice bubbling on the water or even hear it. Remember that every batch is different, and the timing will be different – just like sourdough. You'll know it's ready for step 2 when you see those small bubbles arise.

Let's feed those yeasts.

STEP 2: MASH AND FERMENT

Hydrate the rice kōji with 100 ml (3½ fl oz) water.

Remove the rice bags from the jar and put aside. Strain the rice from the water, carefully keeping the water – this is your brew. Pour the water back into the jar and add the rice kōji.

Now steam the soaked rice until just soft (see page 76). Cool it down to body temperature (by laying it on a mat, perhaps) and then add to the jar.

With very clean hands, massage the cooled steamed rice and the rice kōji together in the jar. Spend some time doing this. It's a chance to put some intention in there again.

Gently empty the little wrapped balls of rice to sit atop this mash. If you've used a cloth bag you can dry it out and keep it for next time; it will hold some lovely bacteria ready to reactivate.

Lid or cover your brew with cloth. Don't worry if it seems a bit like porridge. Do not be tempted to add any water at this stage: you will get a weak and insipid brew. Trust the process – the enzymes will start to break down the rice, and once you strain the solids out, you'll find there's plenty of liquid.

Keep the glass jar at room temperature, but away from direct sunlight. Try to spend about a minute a day stirring or massaging your mash. Taste daily. You will notice it changing from being very sweet to slightly sour and more alcoholic as the ferment proceeds. You'll also notice the level of the mash rising, full of air and life, after a couple of days. Plunge it down with a wooden spoon or a stick.

Usually, this batch size will require 3–5 days of fermentation in warm weather and up to 14 days in cool temperatures. Readiness will depend on these variables – and your preference. Remember that fermentation can be stopped at any stage by placing the brew in a refrigerator and cooling it to around 4°C (39°F).

To bottle, first make sure your bottles are super clean. If keeping some of the rice in your brew (doburoku), stir the mash in the jar, then pour into bottles, using a funnel.

My preference is to strain the brew. First, pour it into a jug through a lined strainer. Squeeze the cloth to extract any liquid into the jug, then pour the strained liquid into bottles. Lid, label and refrigerate. Store upright in your fridge.

Keep the leftovers – the sake lees – in a container in the fridge or freezer. See pages 202–11 for just a few of the many uses for the lees.

When it's time to drink, make sure to open with care as your bottled raw and wild sake can be quite fizzy. Open by gently tilting the bottle to mix the sediment into the brew. Then open slightly, to de-gas, then quickly close, repeating until the sake is settled enough and ready to open fully. Or have your glass ready and just pour and enjoy your fresh brew. This is not the kind of sake that I would consider warming; it is better enjoyed cold.

NOTES: If you are using fresh kōji you will need 400 g (14 oz). If you're making your own kōji, start making it after you prepare the rice water; the two should be ready at the same time. See pages 77–80.

If you're thinking ahead, keep the water you cooked the rice in. Even better, cook it in extra water so it can be used in a rough rice beer (page 73) or fermented for hair rinses (page 215).

You might want to use plastic bottles so you can see the effervescence build as the bottle bulges and won't need to worry about explosions.

The alcohol in this home-brew sake will sit at 6–12% ABV. This is very different to water kefir, ginger beers and kombucha; there is no question, this isn't for kids or those who can't drink alcohol. If you are after the health benefits and the flavours of this brew, but not the alcohol, have a look instead at the recipe for Ama-zake (page 72). Kids love the sweet warmth of it.

```
WARMED SAKE (KANZAKE)

Warming sake can certainly round out rough edges and mask flaws, which
might be a plus for some home-brews. Some sakes are made expressly to be
enjoyed warm, the heat enhancing their aroma, sweetness, sourness and
bitterness. Sake will be called something different depending on how and
to what temperature it is warmed.

In Japan, sake is served cold through to almost scalding. I have always
enjoyed it quite hot - called 'atsukan', which is heated to around 50°C
(122°F). Kanzake is served in a little vase-like jug called a tokkuri,
with small cups called choko.

Some put their tokkuri (porcelain flask) in the microwave to heat the sake,
but a water bath is gentler. Sit the tokkuri into a container or pot of
just-boiled water, making sure that almost all of the vessel is under water.
Leave it until you see bubbles, or until the sake is at 50°C (122°F). Take
it out carefully and enjoy; but, beware: when you drink warmed sake, the
alcohol is absorbed into the body quite quickly. This can actually be good
though, right, as you will know sooner, rather than later, when you've
had enough.
```

AMA-ZAKE (SWEET SAKE)

Prep. 1 hour | Fermentation time: overnight |
Equipment: rice cooker (or slow cooker), thermometer, bottle or jar

Ama-zake is a naturally sweet rice drink which can also be used as a sweetener in dishes. It can be made using other grains, such as oats, or groats, chestnut and other nut meals, quinoa and polenta, or from residual sake lees (page 202). Although fairly plain to look at, this creamy looking brew is a powerful energy drink, packed with good gut bacteria.

Drink ama-zake thinned down a little, blended or enjoy it warm in a bowl as a porridge or gruel with nuts and perhaps some chewy sour fruit on top.

INGREDIENTS

```
200 g (7 oz) rice (short-grain or
  medium-grain or a combination of
  the two)
700 ml (23½ fl oz) warm water
200 g (7 oz) rice kōji
```

First, cook the rice in a pot or rice cooker according to the packet directions, then cool to at least 60°C (140°F). Add the water, crumble in the rice kōji and stir to combine.

You want to keep the mixture at a constant temperature of about 60°C (140°F). It's important to keep it at this temperature – the amylase enzyme is deactivated when the temperature gets too hot; when it is too low the amylase cannot activate properly. I do this by keeping the rice cooker on the 'warm' setting with the lid ajar and a tea towel covering the top; I set it in the evening, leaving it overnight, to wake to the beautiful aroma of ama-zake. A slow cooker set to the same temperature, a yoghurt maker or a multi-cooker will also do the job.

Pour into a bottle or jar. Stored well, this will keep in the fridge for a few months. To keep it stable and the flavour and enzymes intact, you can store it in the freezer for up to 6 months.

NOTES: Try putting ama-zake into an ice-cube tray so you can grab a cube for smoothies, to sweeten baking or to use as a starter culture.

OTHER IDEAS

Ama-zake is delicious on its own but it hosts all kinds of flavours very well.

MASALA CHAI AMA-ZAKE

Combine about 1 teaspoon masala chai spices and 250 ml (8½ fl oz/ 1 cup) water in a saucepan to make an infused tea. Strain, cool a little and add to the rice before overnight fermentation. An even quicker way is to put a couple of tablespoons of ama-zake into a cup and then pour the hot masala chai over it, letting the ama-zake act like the milk *and* the sweetener. So good.

NUTTY AMA-ZAKE PUDDING

Swirl a measure of amaretto, nocino or any slightly bitter nutty liquor over a serve of ama-zake. Add a generous amount of toasted and crushed almonds, pecans, walnuts or hazelnuts for crunch. Enjoy with a fruity black coffee.

A ROUGH RICE BEER

If you are boiling rice for any purpose, for example to make the balls for your sake, boil the rice in a saucepan with what would normally be too much water - say 2 litres (68 fl oz/8 cups) for 100 g (3½ oz) rice - until the rice is cooked. Strain and set the rice aside for other uses. Cool the rice water and pour it into a couple of bottles. Add some flavour and a little something sweet: some lemon and grated ginger, a couple of raisins and a teaspoon of sugar. Lid and gently shake the bottle. Place in a warm spot in your home.

Keep an eye on it for bubbles. Taste it after 2 days; depending on what you've added, your rice water will ferment into a very rough sour 'beer', reminiscent of a Hoegaarden sour beer. Refrigerate promptly as it's quite active. Drink chilled - it may be so fizzy that you'll need care and patience to open it.

Beware. I haven't had this happen in a long time, but while making this recipe for this book I exploded a bottle. I heard it go and ran downstairs to see. Of all the amazing, very active and yeasty drinks I had on the shelf the last thing I expected to blow was this rice water beer, so keep an eye on the pressure.

KŌJI – ENZYME MAGIC

Kōji is the mould responsible for the incredible base flavours in miso, shoyu, tamari, sake and mirin. Kōji is considered Japan's national fungus and comes in many varieties; the main one used for basic and general fermenting is *Aspergillus oryzae*. You'll see other species of the *Aspergillus* genus used for growing kōji but far and away the most popular – and recommended for these recipes – is *A. oryzae*.

The word kōji is used to refer to the actual mould, as well as when the substrate (usually rice) is inoculated with the mould. The spores or seeds are called kōji-kin or tane-kōji and once they are grown on a substrate like rice or barley, for example, it is called rice kōji or barley kōji. If you buy the tane or kōji kin then you will be growing the kōji on a substrate yourself. If you buy the rice kōji it will be ready to use in a ferment straight away.

You can buy rice kōji ready to brew and I recommend doing that to start off with. It's available online or in your Asian food store, on the shelf (dried) or in the fridge or freezer. It will look like opaque dried grain and is packaged differently depending on the maker. It will usually come with recipes or instructions of some kind.

Growing your own kōji at home is very satisfying and isn't more difficult than growing your own sourdough mother and turning that into bread: mould wants to grow, after all. It is just a matter of a little preparation and setting up a system that provides humidity and heat – and a few days of being around to check on it.

THE THING ABOUT KŌJI

With growing kōji comes an addictive, alluring aroma that will lift your heart as you enter the room to check on it and touch you somewhere between your olfactory senses and your tummy; like feeling butterflies. I can't quite explain it but when I enter the room where my makeshift kōji incubator sits, the aroma gives me a little zing of excitement that is perhaps akin to seeing a person you have a crush on walking toward you in the hallway at high school … or any time. Let's be honest, making kōji is worthwhile for a little hit of that now and then. I think so.

It used to be that each miso or sake house grew their own *Aspergillus oryzae*. Over the years, new ways of growing the fungus and higher, tighter standards were developed to the point that there are only a small group of spore companies in Japan now, and the current standards dictate that spores need to be supplied by them.

Rice, barley and soybeans are traditional as a substrate, but you can experiment by growing kōji on all kinds of grains and beans. When it comes to making sake, rice kōji is generally what you're after, so this recipe will show you how to grow kōji onto the substrate of white short-grain rice.

RICE: WASH, SOAK, DRY, STEAM

Rice is an amazing substrate for brewing. Starch galore. Outwardly, it's a simple grain, but its preparation in the brewing and fermenting world is taken very seriously indeed. There are four vital steps for rice: wash, soak, dry (a kind of malting), then steam.

1. Wash Washing your rice until the water runs clear is probably one of the most important parts to kōji growing, makgeolli brewing, sake making – in fact, whenever you cook or ferment rice. Rinsing well is the secret to steaming a perfect bowl of rice. You'll hear it said that rice needs to be washed 100 times. Mine's a waterwise adaptation, but a meditative process nonetheless.

Pour the rice into a suitable container, with room for movement. It is handy if the container sits in your sink and you have a strainer over a clean bucket on the bench next to you. Cover the rice with fresh water – straight from the tap – then, with clean hands and a gentle mind, start to swirl and rub the rice together, over and over until the water is cloudy. Strain the water out into a bucket if you're keeping the water for fermenting or other uses (see page 215), or tip it down the sink. Fill with fresh water again and repeat between 5–10 times – keep going, gently washing the rice until the water runs clear.

2. Soak Soaking will awaken the grain and allow the rice to absorb water better, so it cooks more evenly; it will make more of a difference than you might think. Do whatever works with your schedule, but aim for overnight and even throughout the next day, anywhere from 2–24 hours.

Soaking is akin to sprouting or germination, which is a step of malting grain for beer. Grains for beer require sprouting and, as a basic step, so does makgeolli; rice kōji and its peers also need this step. It's not like soaking nuts or legumes to rid them of phytates – soaking your rice is indeed a malting step.

After washing, cover the rice with about 2.5 cm (1 in) water and sit it somewhere cool where it won't be disturbed. I cover it with a large swathe of muslin (cheesecloth) or a large lid which fits my pot beautifully.

It's a lovely thing to lift the cover and see the water still clear, like a limpid stream, the rice like rocks beneath.

3. Drain/Dry When you are ready, drain your rice (keep this water for fermenting, as above) and sit it in the strainer in a spot where it will breathe somewhat. I often leave the rice overnight, but don't leave it for too long as it might spoil. There's nothing saying you couldn't aim to sprout your rice: Terada Honke does a sprouted brown rice sake that is super delicious.

Not only can you save the starchy water for washing your face and hair, you can also keep it to ferment into a rough rice beer (page 73).

4. Steam Bamboo or metal stacking steamers that sit on top of your saucepan in layers are cheap to buy and give the best results in steaming rice that doesn't stick together. I would never use a rice cooker to make my rice kōji; steaming is the recommended method.

You'll need some fabric to line the steamer; ideally, it'll be a lovely muslin, hemp, linen or cotton sheet. Cut it to fit your steamer base, leaving enough overhang to fold over and cover the rice.

Wet the lining cloth and wring it out. Line each steamer tray with cloth. Add the rice (post wash, soak and dry), dividing it equally among the baskets and spreading it evenly to about 2–4 cm (¾–1½ in) thick.

Fill the saucepan below the steamer with enough water to last the cooking time. It's best to add the layers one by one, giving a bit of time for the first layer to start before adding the second layer so they cook evenly. Steam the rice until al dente. It should take between 40–60 minutes from the first steam. Check after 45 minutes: the rice should be cooked less than you would for eating but it should be glossy, moist and chewy. If you massage a teaspoonful between your thumb and finger for a minute it should also have a small amount of stretch, more so if you are using glutinous rice.

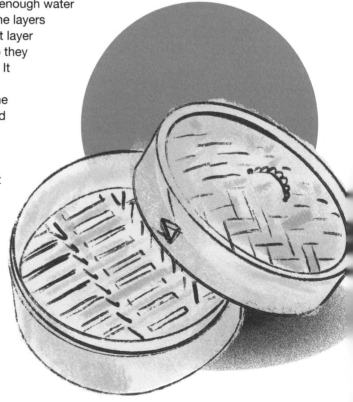

Done. Now you have perfectly prepared rice to grow kōji on.

GROWING KŌJI

Prep. 3-30 hours | Growing time: 3-4 days | Equipment: steamer, tea strainer, muslin (cheesecloth), thermometer, heat source, humidifier, humidity measure

There are quite a few steps to growing kōji. To start with you will need to buy the *Aspergillus oryzae* spores, known as seed kōji or kōji starter. You can find packets of this at specialty stores or with a quick online search for sellers in your area.

Patience, curiosity and a Zen attitude are desirable in this project. Set aside time for the cooking and first incubation period. You then need to be focused and have some room cleared to cool the rice down and get the seed kōji rubbed through the rice. Allow time for peaceful checking and waiting.

INGREDIENTS

1 kg (2 lb 3 oz) short-grain
  white rice, preferably organic
2-5 g (¾-1¾ teaspoons) seed kōji
  (see Note)
1 tablespoon lightly toasted rice
  flour (optional)

NOTE: Seed kōji is usually sold in 10 g (¼ oz) or 20 g (¾ oz) packets. You will need about 2 g (¾ teaspoon) of seed kōji per kilo of rice depending on the strength of the spores – pay attention to the directions on the packet and also to how it blooms once inoculated; you may need to use more or less in future. Some kōji-kin comes with the rice flour mixed in already.

STEP 1: PREPARE (3–30 HOURS)

The important first step is to prepare your rice by washing, soaking, drying and steaming (page 75).

STEP 2: INOCULATE (16–24 HOURS; CHECK AFTER 8)

Carefully measure out 2 g (¾ teaspoon) of seed kōji into a bowl. As with all moulds, take care not to breathe the spores in. Combine with cooled toasted rice flour, if using. (Toasting in a dry pan will kill any existing bacteria or moulds in the flour that might interfere with the kōji.) Blending with rice flour is useful to assist with distribution of such a tiny amount of spores. Add the seed kōji to a small, fine tea strainer or shaker, ready for sprinkling.

Spread the still-warm prepared rice evenly across a clean sheet of cloth, turning the rice over itself as you go. Keep moving the rice so it doesn't clump. When the rice feels warm but not hot, carefully sprinkle the seed kōji over it, quite close to the rice so you don't lose any of the vital spores. Each grain needs to come into contact with a spore, so mix it thoroughly and quickly, with the rice still warm and moist.

Pile the rice up into a pyramid (with the remote thermometer probe in the middle, if using) and bundle the cloth around it. We are aiming to create an environment that is snug, not drying, and also heat inducing. Wrapping the rice will hold it together and help build warmth, similar to a compost heap. I often put the cloth bundle into a second cotton bag. Place your bundle in an incubator. I like to use an esky/cooler, sitting my bundle on a wooden chopping board or tray, with two hot water bottles on either side. The ideal temperature for the mould to flourish is 34–42°C (93–108°F). See Note below.

Wait. Come back in 8 hours if you can, to check on the environment, refill the hot water bottles, and check that the rice isn't too hot or cold. Leave the kōji in this incubation phase for 16–24 hours. At the point that your kōji becomes too warm, you'll need to pull it out and go to Step 3.

A NOTE ON TEMPERATURE: I have recommended you incubate your kōji at the rather high temperatures listed above because this encourages more amylase enzymes, which will turn the starches in the rice into sugar, giving the sweeter flavour we are looking for in sake. As this is a book about drinks, we are making kōji to make sake, but if you are making kōji for miso, then a lower temperature range – from between 27–34°C (80–93°F) – is better, as you are after more protease enzymes. If you want a more savoury sake, the lower range is also fine.

STEP 3: TRAY (10 MINS)

You can use all sorts of trays for this step: lasagne dishes, or vessels made from plastic, stainless steel or glass. They need to be rectangular with a height of about 3 cm (1 in). The rice will need to be spread out evenly and to a depth that will hold heat: no less than 2.5 cm (1 in). You may need several trays. I have recently acquired some beautifully handmade wooden trays – no nails or glue – that really enhance my growing life. They need to be able to fit into your incubator.

First, carefully unwrap the warm rice bundle on your bench, spreading the rice out across the cloth gently with your hands to inspect it. There should be signs of white on the rice, and a lovely, sweet, perhaps fruity chestnut-like aroma. Heaven! Don't panic if you don't get that smell, it might still be OK. Continue gently mixing the rice, checking there aren't any clumps, overly moist edges or dry surface areas.

Distribute the rice kōji onto your clean and dry trays and pop them back, uncovered, into your incubator. Make sure the rice doesn't dry out; depending on what your set-up is, you may need a bowl of water on the bottom and top trays. Trays will go side by side or stacked; either way, make sure there is still airflow between them.

OPPOSITE: SPRINKLING KŌJI
SPORES OVER STEAMED RICE

Insert the thermometer and humidity measure, if using, into the rice on one of the trays, close up the incubator and tweak the environment so it gradually reaches 38–42°C (100–108°F). Leave the rice kōji for another 6–10 hours to develop, only pottering to adjust the temperature or wipe down the surfaces of your incubator if it is too moist. At the 10-hour point, check the rice if you can. This is where you might mix the rice again with a clean hand to make sure the top isn't drying out. With your fingers, gently draw in some 'Zen garden' lines – down the length of the trays or in a circular pattern – to create more surface area for cooling and airflow in general. The rice kōji should certainly smell sweet by now and you should be able to see the white spores on the rice easily.

Close the incubator, then check the temperature and humidity again after 6 hours. After 12 hours, the rice grains should be melded together somewhat and very sweet smelling. Every grain should be entirely white at this stage, and the grains should have little hairs on them – like a mould – some more, some less.

A note on further growth: If you leave the rice kōji just sitting there, or keep it in the incubator for too long, it will keep sporulating, so you need to stop it here. If it keeps growing, you'll see a colour change – new spores are yellow. While this is indeed how you might cultivate your own spores for later use, there can be dangers in trying to capture your own; even the most experienced home kōji growers have told me that they have had their own batches tested to find *Aspergillus flavus* – toxic for human consumption – in their kōji. I recommend buying the pre-tested, certified and lab-made *A. oryzae* spores for the home set-up – and make sure you catch the kōji in time before this next stage of maturation.

STEP 4: USE OR STORE

At this stage, you can use your kōji straight away for a batch of miso, sake or shio-kōji, or store it for later use. To store, put the rice kōji in a container or plastic bag and freeze it, or dry it out further by spreading it very thinly and leaving it out in the sun or in a warm room. In my home in Melbourne, we don't need to dehydrate rice kōji, but in cooler or humid places you should use a dehydrator at about 32°C (90°F) and dry overnight. Keep the kōji in a sealed container in the freezer for longevity. It will freeze well for months.

GRAIN TEAS AND WATERS

Refreshing either hot or cold, these teas are all rather nostalgic, even if you didn't have them as a child. They aren't fermented, but they are still wild drinks – boiled drinks were traditionally a way to make water safe to drink. They were flavoured with what was at hand, and it turns out they are so good for you.

The following grain-brewed waters are popular and traditional all over Asia and you can often buy the grains pre-roasted, ready to brew, in your Asian food store or online. If you can't find them, roast or toast your own.

I recommend using a teapot with a wide opening and a strainer inside to hold the bulkier grains when brewing. For a cold drink, simply bring the grains to a boil in a saucepan of water and then let them continue to steep overnight and strain the tea into a jug for the fridge.

You could ferment these teas using any of the methods in this book, adding some to a kombucha, jun, water kefir, makgeolli, mead or wild soda.

ROASTED BARLEY TEA

Known as bori cha in Korea and mugi-cha in Japan, this is an easy and soothing tea, loaded with antioxidants. I like to make a little extra of this tea to add to my kombucha brewed with a smoky lapsang tea and dried orange peel. Yum. You can buy the grain already roasted in most Asian food stores, but doing it yourself is half the fun.

INGREDIENTS

```
3-4 tablespoons organic pearl barley
2 litres (68 fl oz/8 cups) water
```

To roast or toast the barley, soak it in water, pat dry and then either roast in a 160–200°C (320–390°F) oven – depending on your oven and how toasty you want it – or toast in a dry frying pan over a low heat. In both oven and frying pan, move the grain around frequently, keep an eye on it and take it off the heat when it is brown (about 10 minutes).

Bring the water to a boil, add the barley and simmer for 5 minutes over a medium heat. Remove from the heat and strain out the barley. This tea can be served hot or cold.

LEMON BARLEY WATER

When I was at school, my mum often made lemon barley water in the summer to take for sports days or excursions. It's refreshing and satiating, particularly on hot days.

INGREDIENTS

```
150 g (5½ oz) organic pearl barley
2 litres (68 fl oz/8 cups) water
60 g (2 oz) caster sugar
juice and zest of 3 lemons
```

Rinse the barley in plenty of cold water. Bring the cooking water to the boil in a large saucepan, add the barley, sugar, lemon zest and juice. Simmer, lid on, for 30–45 minutes. Remove from the heat and leave to cool. Strain out the barley, reserving it for other uses (soups, breads, salads, etc.). Taste and adjust with more sugar and lemon juice as desired. Pour into a jug or bottle, refrigerate and serve any time.

NOTE: You can also add a ginger beer mother (page 130) to the lemon barley water and let it ferment for a sparkling, living drink.

TOASTED CORN TEA

Toasted corn tea is widely enjoyed in Korea, known as oksusu-cha. Gentle on your gut, you can happily drink this all day on an empty stomach or enjoy it with food. This lightly sweet and thirst-quenching brew is more often enjoyed warm in the winter, but can also be refrigerated and served cold. It makes a good cocktail base and is a delicious addition to kombucha.

INGREDIENTS

```
50 g (1¾ oz/¼ cup) fresh corn
  kernels
1.5 litres (51 fl oz/6 cups) water
```

Place the corn kernels in a dry frying pan over a low heat, moving them around to toast. You want the corn kernels to be a deep golden brown, even charred in places, and hard and dry before making tea from them.

Combine the water and corn in a saucepan and bring to the boil. Simmer for about 20 minutes. Taste and add more water if desired. It will taste pleasingly and moreishly like corn and summer.

OTHER CORN TEAS

Save the corn silks themselves when you first prepare a cob; apparently, there is one strand of silk per kernel – isn't that magical? Keep the precious threads and dry them out on a windowsill between some paper or by just sitting them in the sun. You can also brew them fresh with the kernels. This tea is great for things like lowering your blood pressure and flushing out toxins. Simply use one corn cob's worth of silk per cup of boiling water, brewed in a small teapot for a super quick, frugal and pure tea.

An easy way to enjoy a kind of 'corn tea' is simply to drink the cooking water from your boiled corn on the cobs: strain, pour into a cup and serve immediately. With a few additional seasonings, it becomes a pure, savoury bouillon. Some of the simplest things are the most memorable and nurturing.

PANDAN AND JOB'S TEARS WATER

This grain-of-many-names is not pearl barley, even though you'll see it translated as such. Job's tears is a gluten-free millet, a much smaller grain than barley. It's easily found in Asian food stores as Chinese pearl barley. Job's tears is used in all kinds of drinks in Asia and it also appears widely in folk medicine as well as traditional Chinese medicine. Look into it – it imparts a beautiful sweet nutty flavour reminiscent of oatmeal.

INGREDIENTS

```
200 g (7 oz) Job's tears (millet)
2 litres (68 fl oz/8 cups) water
150 g (5½ oz) palm or coconut sugar
2 pandan leaves, rinsed and knotted
1 lemon, sliced
honey, to taste
```

Wash the grains in running water until the water runs clear. Combine the grains with the cooking water in a saucepan and bring to the boil over a medium heat. Reduce the heat, cover and simmer for about 45 minutes, or until the grain is soft. Add the sugar and pandan leaves and simmer for a few minutes, stirring occasionally until the sugar has dissolved. Take off the heat, add the lemon and let cool. Taste and add honey to sweeten if desired. Remove the pandan leaves.

This can be consumed immediately, with or without the grains, or strained and bottled.

NOTE: Enjoy this drink cold. If you'd like to ferment it, you could use a yeast starter, such as a ginger beer mother (page 130). Add it while the brew is still at body temperature and feed the yeast some sugar. I would add about 2–4 tablespoons ginger beer starter and sugar to 1 litre (34 fl oz/4 cups) tea. Bottle, lid and leave to sit on the bench for a day or until you get some fizz. Refrigerate.

BUCKWHEAT TEA (SOBA-YU)

Many soba houses in Japan will give you a pot with the water that the noodles were cooked in to drink. It's so delicious and nurturing. There's a reason to drink this water too – a lot of nutrients leach into the water during cooking. The soba-yu (simply translated as soba water) contains several excellent beneficial nutrients including water-soluble chemicals, such as rutin (an antioxidant), and B vitamins. Next time you make yourself some soba, hold back some of the soba-yu to try.

DANDELION ROOT BREW

This recipe is all about the dandelion plant's roots (rather than featuring a grain) and it shares the roasty/toasty vibe of a coffee. Dandelion foraging is very satisfying, but you do need to make sure you have the right plant – there are lookalikes. True dandelions have perfect fluffy seed heads, with leaves and stalks that release a milky sap when cut. The flower stalks rise straight up out of the centre – one flower per stalk – and the hairless leaves are deeply toothed and can grow up to 25 cm (9 in) long. The strong taproot can be hard to dig out; it's easier to cut out when the soil is moist. Look for large flowers to guide you to larger roots: you are going to need about 10 roots to make this project worthwhile. Pull the leaves off to use in salads and green smoothies, dry them for tea or use in Dandelion wine (pages 96–7).

Wash the roots several times. You will probably need to use a brush or scouring pad to get all the dirt off. Remove the little side roots. Dehydrate overnight at 38°C (100°F) or put the roots between two wads of newspaper for a few days. Cut the roots into small pieces and roast in a 180°C (350°F) oven, with the door ajar, for 30 minutes. Chop the roots into even smaller pieces and roast for another 30 minutes, door closed this time. Be careful not to burn the roots: when they are dry and brown, they are ready.

Grind the roots with a mortar and pestle or in a coffee grinder. The result will look like coffee. Dandelion coffee does not dissolve, so use a coffee plunger or a tea strainer if you have one. Otherwise, bring to a boil in a saucepan and strain out as you would a chai masala. Use about 2–3 teaspoons per cup. This goes well with milk and honey.

Ferment

FERMENT

SIMPLE FERMENTS

Not every ferment in this book requires a SCOBY, heat, malt, sprouting or other more complex techniques. The recipes in this chapter rely on things such as apples and honey, flowers and vegetables, peels, rhubarb, sugar and good water: things you can find in your pantry, in a supermarket, or on a farm or field.

I hope this chapter fosters experimentation, maybe new farmers' market finds, or a bit of veggie or medicinal herb garden growing. In the past I've made some lovely (and some not so good) wines from pea pods, from carrots and even from parsnip and prune. I've dabbled with apples, blackberries, cherries, peaches, plums, raspberries, rhubarb, strawberries – so many choices. You can blend fruit and add teas for tannin, or try adding roasted grain teas (see page 82) for complexity. Sometimes, you'll think something is not working out, but if you just leave it a little longer, it will. Keep tasting and testing.

Choosing fruits that have exposed yeasts yields the best results. The yeast is the white bloom you can see on the skin, particularly on dark fruits such as plums, grapes, tomatoes and even feijoa. The wild yeast is there, quietly waiting for the skin to break so it can dive in and help to rot the fruit. Because we are setting the fruit up in the right environment to become soured through the lactic acid bacteria and to welcome the yeasts in, we don't have to worry about rot. We are, however, treading a fine line between wine and vinegar, and delicious or … kind of not.

STRAINING BEET KVASS

A NOTE ON YEASTS AND ADDITIVES

Of all the different yeasts that exist in this world, our dearest friend is the *Saccharomyces* genus. From the nineteenth century, yeasts were grown for specific purposes, and since then, winemakers have had access to an increasing number of varieties, depending on the taste and aroma profile they seek. More recently, the over-commercialisation of winemaking has led some makers back to basics. The traditional methods haven't been lost, and they seem to be in fashion again – how great is that?

Wild yeasts – which are everywhere – are very different to commercial yeasts, just like a wild animal is different to one that's been born and raised in captivity. The wild textures and flavours can be more complex, but also unpredictable: they haven't been bred in a lab for a specific purpose. I think it's fun to play with wild yeasts – in some ways, they are our last frontier … and right there in the kitchen!

Using Campden tablets (adding sulfites) is common practice in larger-scale fermenting, and now also with regular home fermenting. People use sulfites to inhibit bacteria and the growth of wild yeasts, and sulfites are also used to eliminate chlorine and chloramine from treated mains water. Campden tablets contain sodium metabisulfite and don't affect flavour. While they won't kill all wild bacteria, they kill acetobacter, which makes vinegar. If you'd like to use Campden tablets, a typical use is one crushed tablet per 4 litres (135 fl oz) of must, wort or water. I don't use a lot of sulfites, but there is a place for them, particularly if you aren't sure about the water you are using.

Citric acid is often used to provide acidity and might be needed when the fruit you use doesn't supply enough. I prefer to use lemon juice or peel over citric acid.

Yeast nutrient is something to feed the yeast; usually, your brew will contain enough of that, but there are nutrients you can buy, or you can try making extra yeast. Recently, I've started to add a small amount of yeast here and there as I make larger batches. It's up to you.

Tannin can help to keep ferments fresh-tasting and astringent. The tannin that keeps our pickles crunchy comes from vine leaves. You can add blackberry, raspberry, cherry or tea leaves to get tannin. Floral wines and simple brews can be given depth this way.

My experience with fermenting started with an appreciation of the magic of wild fermentation. As a person who loves to cook and understand ingredients, why had most kitchen practices in my life not included the day-to-day use of fermentation? Why had fermentation been replaced by relying solely on refrigerators and freezers, and why had the kitchen become a place for cooking only? It was the magic that drew me. Adding yeasts, sulfites, nutrients and bacteria takes some of that away for me. Almost comparable to making a cake with a packet mix. It's going to be moist and it's going to be delicious, but do you feel amazing when you make it, or are you just glad to have a cake? Do you feel proud when people compliment you on that cake? No. It's a different feeling with wild versus packets for fermenting for me as well.

OPPOSITE: STRAINING RHUBARB FIZZ

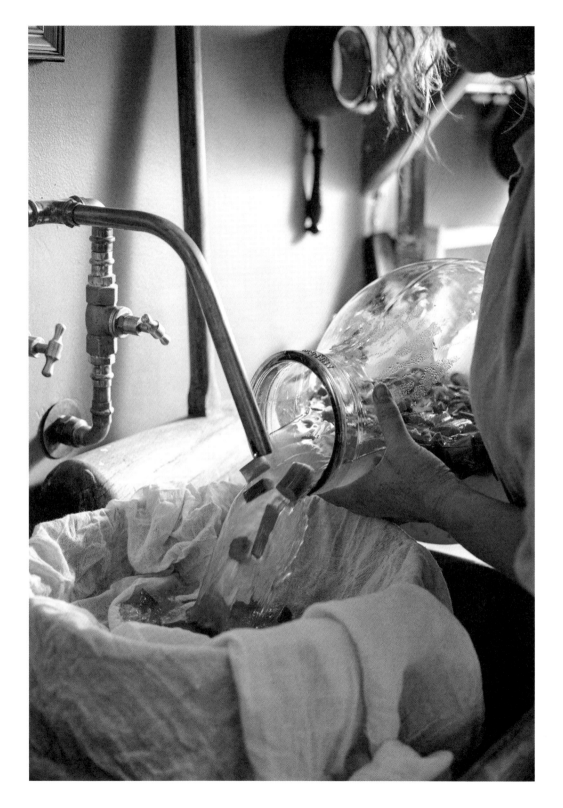

RHUBARB FIZZ

Prep. 10 minutes, plus 1 hour sitting time | Fermentation time:
3-5 days | Equipment: 2 L (68 fl oz) jar, muslin (cheesecloth),
bottles

This is a gorgeous, sweet, tart fizz that can get slightly boozy. Rhubarb is great for your gut and has been used medicinally for thousands of years. I craved it in all its forms all through my pregnancies and beyond.

INGREDIENTS

300 g (10½ oz) chopped rhubarb
  (about a bunch)
250 g (9 oz) fine sugar
splash of vinegar (white wine,
  apple cider or kombucha)
juice of ½ lemon
2 litres (68 fl oz/8 cups) water

Freeze and thaw the rhubarb if you have time – it'll bring out the flavour a little more.

Place the rhubarb in the jar with the sugar, vinegar and lemon juice and leave to macerate for an hour. Add the water and stir well.

Cover with a cloth and leave for 3–5 days, stirring now and again and checking on the flavour. When it is no longer too sweet and is slightly effervescent (and before it turns too sour), prepare to bottle.

Strain through a cloth over a sieve, gathering up the fruit and squeezing it to get as much liquid out of the rhubarb as possible. Reserve the spent fruit for other uses (see Note). Pour into good-quality bottles. You can add complexity at this stage by adding a few coffee beans and vanilla, or a handful of rose petals, for example. Lid your brew.

Leave out on a bench to develop fizziness – depending on your brew, it will take anywhere from a day to a week. If keeping an eye on it is inconvenient, let it age in the refrigerator.

NOTE: You can store the spent rhubarb in a 2% brine to eat like a pickle, or cook it up with some sugar and apples until soft. Serve with yoghurt or in pies.

DANDELION WINE

Prep. 30 minutes | Fermentation time: 1-2 weeks | Equipment: large
bucket, vessel or tub (see Note), cloth, 5 L (170 fl oz) fermenter
with airlock, siphon, bottles (flip-top preferably)

The flavour of this traditional ferment is mild and subtle, yet evokes the
taste of sunshine – the sleepy feeling and aromas when you rest your head
on the grass, and a touch of chamomile. Can you taste it? It tastes like the
smell of a summer afternoon. Light and evocative.

I still carry a very romantic view of this wine due to Ray Bradbury's
nostalgic book *Dandelion Wine*. I read it when I was fourteen, living in
Kuala Lumpur, and the book has stayed with me ever since. I loved its old-
fashioned view of life in small town America; I also made my first pineapple
wine that year in science class.

Dandelions are an extremely useful plant. This 'weed' has been used in
traditional medicine by humans throughout our history. If you can manage
to pick the whole plant, including the root, you can use the petals for this
wine, dry the leaves for dandelion tea and clean the roots and roast them
for a coffee-like brew (page 87) – *all* of the dandelion has health-giving
properties. It grows prolifically, just waiting to be used.

Hopefully you will know of a place where you can pick dandelions that
have not been sprayed with anything. Pick the flowers in the morning

when they are fully open – the sooner you get them home and into water or the freezer the better. Before that, you need to carefully pluck all the yellow petals off, avoiding any green or white, and get brewing lickety-split: you don't want the petals turning brown and bitter. I have a bag in the freezer that I add petals to until I have enough (pull the petals off before freezing though). If collecting them is too much, you can source dried leaves from herbalists and tea companies.

INGREDIENTS

4 litres (135 fl oz) water
4 litre tub (135 fl oz) loosely
  packed dandelion petals

After 3 days

2 organic oranges, thinly sliced
2 organic lemons, thinly sliced
1 kg (2 lb 3 oz) white sugar
125 ml (4 fl oz/½ cup) wild yeast
  starter, such as ginger beer
  mother (page 130) or 2.5 g
  (½ sachet) champagne yeast
250 g (9 oz) organic light/golden
  raisins

Bring the water to a boil in a large saucepan. Add the petals, reserving a cup to add later. Place this amount in the freezer. Take the pan off the heat, cover with a cloth and leave to sit for 3 days.

Return the liquid to the boil, add the sliced fruit and simmer for 10 minutes. Remove the pan from the heat, add the sugar and stir until dissolved. Let cool to room temperature, then add the yeast, raisins and reserved petals. Transfer to a clean tub, large bowl or wide-mouthed jar and cover with a cloth. Stir daily to make sure the flowers don't form a cap on top. Stir vigorously each time. It should begin to bubble after 3–5 days. Taste it after about 10 days to see if it's becoming less sweet.

After about 10 days, strain the solids out through a lined sieve. Pour the wine into a fermenter with an airlock. Let it sit and ferment longer until the airlock shows only the occasional bubble, almost inactive. Siphon the wine into bottles (see page 32), lid, label and leave somewhere out of the way to age. Six months ageing is perfect in my view, although some people age it for many years.

NOTE: I use a wide-mouthed vessel for the first ferment because it can be difficult to get the petals out of demijohns when you're straining and it ends up being a more annoying job than it needs to be. You can swap out the dandelions for other flowers, such as lilacs, roses or peonies.

BEET KVASS

Prep. 15 minutes | Fermentation time: 3-10 days | Equipment: 3 L
(101 fl oz) jar, muslin (cheesecloth), bottles

Beetroots on their own are highly nutritious, and they are a great vegetable
to ferment with because they have a lot of sugar – in fact, their sugar beet
relatives are a source of commercial sugar production. In kvass, you pull
that sugar out, feed yeast and bacteria with it and get to enjoy a sour,
savoury drink that is full of life and has an awesome colour. You can use the
beetroot in other things (see Notes), but the star here is the liquid.

You're going to crave the tang of this drink perhaps more than other drinks.
I certainly do. I am always seeking out – and love – ingredients, dishes or
drinks that feel as though they are good for my liver. This drink is one of
them; I can feel it doing me good every time.

As with anything steeped in culture and tradition, there are many versions
of beet kvass, some using starter cultures. If you feel the need to speed up
the ferment, you can use whey, ginger beer starter, sauerkraut juice or even
water kefir. I usually let it do its own thing, which will take a bit longer but
makes something a little wilder. See Notes for alternative flavours.

INGREDIENTS

8-10 organic beetroots (beets),
  peeled and cut into chunks
2 pieces orange zest
15 g (½ oz/1 tablespoon) black
  peppercorns
3 bay leaves
2-3 slices fresh ginger
rosemary sprig
pinch of salt
enough good water to fill your jar

Add the beetroot and flavourings to your jar and top with water, leaving a
little headroom. (I pour from a great height and assume it's like stirring –
right?) Cover with cloth and secure. Leave in a warm spot in your kitchen.
Agitate it often – this will thwart the surface-loving, bitter-making yeast
(see Notes).

Taste the kvass at every stirring and note how it develops. The flavour will
sour and it will begin to fizz between 3 and 10 days. At this point – when the
sugars are gone and it's slightly effervescent – bottle.

Strain and pour into clean bottles. Fill to the absolute brim to avoid any yeasts (see Notes) and carbonation build-up. Lid. If you'd like a bit more fizz, leave the bottles out for a day or two. Refrigerate. Beet kvass will keep for months.

NOTES: Kahm yeast is harmless but common in these ferments. It can make your brew bitter, viscous and a little slimy. Avoid it by stirring regularly during fermentation and aim to leave as little air room as possible: fill your jar almost fully – don't use a huge jar and fill only half, for example. Bottle to the brim.

The spent beetroot itself doesn't have a lot of flavour left and can be a bit sour, but I have roasted it with other vegetables – tossed in olive oil, herbs and garlic – which worked well. I've also sautéed it and then added it to smooth dips, such as yoghurt and garlic dip. Delicious.

A tweak I like to make is to add 2 large handfuls of clean, pesticide-free rose petals and 1 sliced orange.

BLACK CARROT KANJI
(GAJAR KI KANJI)

Prep. 10 minutes | Fermentation time: 4-7 days | Equipment: 3-5 L (101-170 fl oz) jar, muslin (cheesecloth), bottles

Salty drinks are commonplace in India, usually super refreshing and often strongly flavoured. This one is served during the spring festival of Holi. Black carrot kanji comes from Rajasthan and the Gujarat and Punjab regions and is a delicious addition to your wild fizz collection. It is often served with sweet chickpeas on top – though that's a step too far for me.

INGREDIENTS

- 1 tablespoon brown mustard seeds, roughly ground
- 1 tablespoon black or fine sea salt
- 1.5 litres (51 fl oz/6 cups) water
- 5 large dark purple carrots, peeled and chopped into batons
- 1-2 small beetroot (beets), peeled and chopped

Combine the mustard, salt and water in the jar and stir vigorously. Add the remaining ingredients. Stir, cover with cloth and secure. Let it sit at room temperature, visiting a couple of times a day to stir.

Once it is sour and slightly fizzy, strain and bottle the liquid, leaving the bottles out a day or two longer to get more fizz if desired. Refrigerate. Enjoy on ice, with food or on its own.

NOTE: Reserve the carrot batons to eat like pickles; if you don't eat them the same day, keep them in some of the juice, covered, in a bowl or jar in the fridge. The kanji liquid can also be used as a marinade for a tasty snack called kanji vada – fritters that are fried and then soaked in the kanji overnight.

COUNTRY WINE – FERMENTING FRUIT TO DRINK

Wine is an ancient drink – just like cider, beer, sake and mead – and we can make small amounts in our kitchens at home without intervention or additives. As with cider, we are simply pressing the fruit and setting it up in the right environment, for the right amount of time, in the same way this has been done for millennia.

Georgia, in Eastern Europe, is getting international attention for its wine today, made using ancient techniques. Many households still ferment a low- to no-intervention wine, some in gorgeous, giant egg-shaped earthenware crocks called qvevri that are buried beneath the ground to age. The grapes are fermented with skins, stalks, pips and all. Evidence of this method of winemaking found in Georgia appears to be more than 8000 years old.

Digging and burying aside, a more accessible container for this fruit wine will do the job: a crock or a large glass jar is great, but if you don't have either, look for a food-grade plastic tub.

FRUIT WINE

Prep. 15 minutes | Fermentation time: 3-7 days | Equipment: 5 L (170 fl oz) crock, bucket or jar, muslin (cheesecloth), bottles

INGREDIENTS

- 1 kg (2 lb 3 oz) soft fruit (see Note)
- 250 g (9 oz) sugar (cane sugar, coconut sugar, honey)
- 2 litres (68 fl oz/8 cups) water
- 1 vine leaf or other tannin-rich leaf (optional; see Notes)

Add the whole fruit to the jar, squishing and smashing it a bit with a masher (or, if you are increasing the recipe amount, then using clean hands or feet is fun too). Add the sugar, water and vine leaf, if using. Cover with a cloth and leave to ferment. Stir well several times a day to mix in your yeasts and feed the brew oxygen. You'll notice a cap of fruit forms on the top – you'll need to push that down to avoid attracting yeasts. Depending on the temperature and the yeasts on the fruit, in a couple of days it will start to froth, then peak and then subside over a couple more days. Taste – you're looking for some fizziness and a good sour and sweet balance. Strain into bottles and refrigerate straight away. It will become fizzier and more delicious, and also slightly alcoholic.

NOTES: Berries or pitted stone fruit are good for fruit wine. I particularly like strawberries; the fruit should be ripe. As mentioned elsewhere, freezing and thawing the fruit before fermenting can bring about a stronger flavour.

Other options to add a little tannin are a few unsprayed blackberry leaves or a cup of brewed tea.

Must is the fresh juice of your fruit that contains the solids (stems, leaves, skins) of the fruit to make your wine. When you strain off the juice to make the wine, the solids you are left with are called the pomace. Throughout our long worldwide history of winemaking, pomace has been used in different ways – distilled into grappa, as a colourant, as syrups and vinegars and as a sweetener.

WINE FROM ONE INGREDIENT – GRAPES

Prep. 30 minutes | Fermentation time: 7-10 days, plus 2-4 weeks | Equipment: 2 L (68 fl oz) crock, fermenter or bucket, refractometer or hydrometer, muslin (cheesecloth), carboy or demijohn with airlock, siphon, bottles | Makes: 1 litre (34 fl oz/4 cups)

It's possible to make a pretty good natural wine at home from grapes – and, like with any recipe, there are many ways to go about it. Quality and freshness of the fruit is paramount. One tip is to try and pick the grapes yourself if you can, or look for a grower who sells grapes picked for home winemakers – try to get hold of them within two days of picking. In any case, with wild fermentation in particular, you'll get the best results if the grapes are perfectly ripe and picked on a dry day so the yeasts are all intact.

INGREDIENTS

1.5 kg (3 lb 5 oz) red or white
grapes

Wash the grapes and remove as many stalks as possible to reduce bitter flavours. In a large bowl or tub, crush and juice the grapes with your hands – or clean feet or a pounder or press – and remove any remaining stems. Pour the crushed grapes and liquid into your fermenting bucket or crock.

Monitor the ferment by taking readings with your refractometer or hydrometer at this stage and note them down. You don't *have* to do this, but it is the only way to ultimately establish the alcohol level and how much sugar has been consumed and how much is still left (see page 29). Cover and secure the crock with a cloth or lid.

At this stage, it's important to stir the wine every day to aerate it. As part of your daily routine, you also need to push down the grapes or skins that have floated to the top. Break up this raft and submerge the solids in the juice; you don't want the exposed fruit to form a solid cap that will attract unwanted yeasts, which can change the ferment and endanger it.

This first stage should take 7–10 days. The ferment will get fizzy as the sugars are converted to alcohol. You'll know it is slowing and ready to transfer to the carboy when the grape skins no longer keep getting pushed to the top by the carbon dioxide – they'll sink to the bottom. Pay attention at this stage because you don't want to go over time or else the wine will start to oxidise. If you measured with the hydrometer to begin with, check again now.

BELLA BUSY STOMPING GRAPES

Strain the liquid, pressing the skins to get as much juice out as possible. For small volumes, this can be done with a large strainer lined with cloth. Use a clean pillow case or large square of cloth to help squeeze all the juice from the skins for large amounts. It will smell good now, like wine. Pour into a carboy or demijohn with an airlock. You don't want too much air space at the top: fill any vessel quite close to the top. Whatever vessel you are using, keep an eye on the liquid and level every week, waiting for the bubbling to stop. This could take 2–4 weeks, or more if the temperature is cool.

When the bubbles have stopped, prepare your bottles and rack the wine with a siphon to avoid the sediment on the bottom (see page 32). Seal and label your bottles, then let them age for a few more months. When you open your wine, it may give off a strong smell; leave those gases to vent for a while – it will still taste good.

HONEY AND MEAD

Raw honey – unprocessed, unpasteurised, unfiltered – is life itself and is just sitting there waiting for its moment. My view is that honey lends itself even better to fermentation than being eaten 'au naturel' or used in cooking. The pleasurable sound of its bubbles in a ferment confirms this for me. You really need to use raw honey for this – pasteurised honey (which has become the norm: the cheapest and most prolific honey about) has had the life heated out of it on purpose.

Honey becomes runnier when fermented and takes on the flavour of whatever you put in there – almost anything you add will be enhanced and glorious. It can also be used as a starter and flavour for your other brews. You might get your herbalist head spinning and make some potions: a soda, a syrup to take by the spoonful, or a saucy drizzle for anywhere you see fit. If you find a combination you like, then you can scale it up and use that concoction in a mead as well. I have a garlic honey ferment that is many years old now, and the garlic cloves are like chewy gorgeous lollies. Ginger does something similar.

Mead, in its simplest form, is made of water and honey. It is a rather miraculous transformation to just add water to a product fresh from your hive and make a sparkling, scintillating drink. Of course, it's ancient – it was almost certainly a happy accident at some point – and to be honest, has had a dubious reputation as a cloyingly sweet tipple at times, but mead has gained popularity again. There are some really nice and lively local meads, and the kind I love is more like a cross between cider and sparkling wine – or a beer, if you add bitter herbs. Mead actually belongs in a category all of its own: not a beer, nor a wine or cider.

In the past, mead was called hydromel. Today, the term hydromel is used, somewhat loosely, to refer to lower alcohol meads.

WILD FERMENTED HONEY

Prep. 10 minutes | Fermentation time: 5+ days | Equipment: small or large jars, with a lid or airlock system (see Note)

TRY RAW HONEY WITH:

– **Garlic and nigella**: peel 10–20 cloves and add a teaspoon of nigella seeds. The mixture of honey, nigella and garlic is a Middle Eastern home remedy said to 'cure everything but death'.

– **Chillies**: use fresh red or jalapeño. Within a couple of weeks, you'll have a warm spicy honey to drizzle over grilled haloumi, pizza or baked potatoes.

– **Ginger, turmeric and black pepper**: grains of paradise pepper are amazing for this. A spoon of this warming honey blend is delicious just in a mug of hot water.

– **Fruit**: chopped nectarines, peaches, blackberries, figs, pomegranate, persimmons or elderberries, for example. I usually like to stick to one variety, essentially making a quick fermented syrup.

– **Echinacea, licorice and spices**: this is an awesome tonic/cough syrup. Combine half a cup each of echinacea and licorice root, a couple of sprigs of thyme, a handful chopped fresh ginger root and a shake of cinnamon.

VARIOUS HONEY FERMENTS, WITH CORN SILK DRYING ON TOP OF THE RIGHT JAR

The ratios in these combinations are up to you – you may decide you'll have more use for the honey than the 'bits'. Place cleaned ingredients (no mouldy bits) into a sterilised jar and cover with raw honey. Leave a bit of headroom in the jar. Seal well. This doesn't need to be a large jar or a massive project. A few slices of nectarine, for example, with a twig of thyme, in a tiny jar, covered in honey, lidded and nurtured, will bring flavour and extended life to the fruit. A small jar with only a couple of chillies would work too.

Every day, for a week, tip the jar over: one day onto its lid, the next day back onto its base and so on. The honey will slowly begin to get runnier and then turn fizzy: when it gets fizzy, 'burp' it by opening and closing the jar quickly every so often. It's nice to be able to pick up your jar, twirl it around like a kaleidoscope and watch the viscosity changing. Your fermented honey (and the infused goodies) will be ready to use in about a week, but if you can wait it will get better with age and can last for years – honey is a great preserver. If you are using an airlock system, you can just leave the honey for a couple of weeks until it has calmed down, then transfer it to a jar and lid it.

NOTES: Your jar doesn't have to be big, but you will get some initial action, some build-up of carbon dioxide. I recommend sitting your jar on a plate, or preferably using an airlock lid to avoid sticky leaks, mess or outright explosions. If you're not using an airlock, remember to burp the jar.

Chilli, garlic or turmeric honey is great for a sweet marinade or to drizzle on carrots with butter, on noodles, rice, dumplings or stir-fried anything, as well as roast vegetables, dahl or plain rice. Fruit honeys are delicious poured over yoghurt, on porridge or crumpets, with cheese or with steamed vegies.

You can use this flavoured and living honey to make a wild soda: add a couple of tablespoons or more of your young fermented honey to a 1 litre (34 fl oz/4 cups) jar of water, add the fruit of your choice and a slice of lemon for acidity, then stir and lid. Let it sit out for a couple of days, shaking it as you go by. It will be sparkling within a few days.

WILD MEAD

Prep. 5 minutes | Fermentation time: 10 days, plus 2 weeks |
Equipment: bucket, crock or large jar, muslin (cheesecloth),
jar with airlock, bottles

A wild fermented mead is simply water and honey, left out to attract yeast.
While I do occasionally add yeast to my mead, I prefer making it without
additional yeast – it's something to do with the purity of the ingredients
and the magic of fermentation at its most innocent.

INGREDIENTS

1 part raw honey (see Notes)
4 parts water
champagne yeast (optional;
  see Notes)

Mix the honey and water in your chosen wide-mouthed vessel and cover
with cloth. Stir vigorously about five times a day, making a decent whirlpool,
then stir in the opposite direction. It's a lovely and traditional thing to use
a porous stick that will catch yeasts, which will remain in the wood if you
allow it to dry. You can then perhaps inoculate your next brew with the stick.
This is a witchy thing – let's not dull that with scientific descriptions! Stir like
this for about 5 days; it will get frothy on top and the aroma wafting up will
be tantalising.

Keep stirring intermittently for another 5 days. When the bubbles start to
ease, strain the mead into a jar with an airlock. Sit it somewhere you won't
forget it and wait until the bubbles in the airlock start to slow – maybe
another week or two. Strain well, bottle, refrigerate and let the mead age in
the fridge for a couple of weeks.

*NOTES: The ratio of honey to water can be adjusted according to your palate. You
may prefer a less sweet ratio of 1:6.*

*As an indication of the alcohol level of this wild mead, mine tested at 12% ABV made
at a 1:4 ratio.*

*After letting a couple of batches go overtime, and running out of uses for the resulting
vinegar, I felt bad about the wasted honey. After all, it came from the hardworking
bees in our backyard hive. In came the champagne yeast. I use it from time to time
and I know it works.*

MEAD VARIATIONS

You can also add fruit, flowers or spices – or a combination – to your mead. The extra yeasts that sit on these additions will impact the ferment, so be aware of that.

When you ferment mead with fruit it is called a melomel, when you add spices it is a metheglin, and with roses or rosehips it's a rhodomel. There are dozens of mead variations, from all over Europe, but I particularly love these lyrical names.

Try any of the below combinations with a honey–water ratio of 1 cup honey to 6 cups water. Use a 2 L (68 fl oz/8 cups) jar.

- 1 or 2 persimmons, unpeeled, sliced; 1 cinnamon stick; 3 dried figs

- 1 thumb-sized piece of fresh ginger, unpeeled, chopped; freshly grated nutmeg; rosemary sprig

- 2 sprigs lavender; 2 sprigs sage; 2 sprigs thyme; ½ tablespoon black pepper

- 1 tablespoon cacao nibs, cracked

IMMUNITY BOOST SYRUP

This is an oxymel (page 162) and hydromel hybrid. With the addition of herbs, spices and fruit, it is rich in antioxidants – and tasty.

```
Prep. 1 hour | Equipment: 1 L (34 fl oz) bottle or jar with lid
```

INGREDIENTS

```
1 litre (34 fl oz/4 cups) water
1 cup fresh elderberries or ½ cup
  dried
2 dried figs
4 dried apricots
1 tablespoon dried astragalus
1 tablespoon dried echinacea root
2 teaspoons grated fresh ginger
approx. ½ cup fresh thyme leaves
  or ¼ cup dried, or to taste
350 g (12½ oz/1 cup) raw honey
½ tablespoon brown rice vinegar
```

Add the water to a saucepan with the elderberries, figs, apricots, astragalus, echinacea, ginger and half the thyme. Bring to the boil, then lower to a simmer, uncovered, for 30 minutes.

Remove from the heat and add the rest of the thyme. Cover and leave to steep for 20 minutes.

Pour the brew through a cloth-lined strainer into a bowl or jug, pressing firmly or gathering the bundle up and squeezing the cloth to get all remaining liquid out. Add the honey, stir to dissolve, then add the vinegar.

Pour the liquid into the bottle or jar and lid it. Refrigerated, it should keep for 6 months. Not only is this a great tonic that can be drunk straight from a little glass or taken by the spoonful like when you were a child, you can also add it to herbal teas, your second ferments, or splash it into a glass of water to drink.

WILD AND WHEY SODAS

A wild soda relies on captured yeasts from other sources for fizz. It requires good unchlorinated water, a touch of fermentable sugar, fruits or botanicals, and time. When you rely on the natural yeasts and bacteria available on the surface of ingredients, every batch will be different, and the flavour might be sourer than you are used to. Rely on nature: choose fruits and botanicals that are known to carry higher levels of yeasts. The white bloom you see on grapes, plums and apples, for example, will give your ferments a head start. It's also present on mint, on spruce tips, young, green pine cones and on wildflowers and roses. Making soda can take a little longer with flowers – it may take 5 days or so – but it's extremely exciting when it comes together and you get the soda-like bubbles.

You can add whey to anything that has a bit of sugar, bottle it and let it ferment. Within days, you'll have made yourself a gorgeous sparkling drink. Adding whey to a store-bought apple juice or something you've juiced yourself is really easy and guaranteed to fizz: simply add the whey, swirl and leave the drink to sit out at room temperature for 2–4 days, then refrigerate.

A reliable ratio for whey soda is to add about 4 tablespoons whey per 500 ml (17 fl oz/2 cups) liquid. You can get living whey by straining milk kefir for labneh and keeping the whey, which is the best for soda, or simply buy yoghurt and strain that for whey. If you have collected whey and aren't ready to use it, freeze it into cubes.

Use any of the following flavour combinations for either a whey soda or wild soda.

BLUEBERRIES IN WHEY SODA

SODA

Prep time: 10-20 minutes | Fermentation time: 3-5 days | Equipment: 2 L (68 fl oz) jar, muslin (cheesecloth), bottles (see Note)

You will need four elements: water + sweetener + wild yeast + flavourings. See below for some delicious ideas on fruit and botanical flavourings.

It's best to use unchlorinated, filtered water: we are aiming to grow bacteria, not kill them off. Rainwater or spring water is good. If not, a good filter will do the trick.

For every 2 litres (68 fl oz/8 cups) water, add ¼–½ cup of honey, sugar or other natural sweetener. When you are experimenting, you should take into account sugars from any fruit or vegetable that you juice and adjust the added sweetener accordingly. The sugar is critical: it is key to getting yeasts eating and burping out the gas that is our fizz. Be careful not to use processed sugar alternatives like stevia, for example, as it is non-fermentable. If you use whey as a starter, you don't need to add as much sweetener.

Wild yeasts are the best sort of uninvited guest. You can rely on wild yeasts to just appear, to gather in the drink by simply leaving the jar out with a loosely woven cloth on top. Or you can grow your own yeast in a substrate first – maybe a Ginger beer mother (page 130) – but allow time for that first step.

FLAVOURINGS

To 2 litres (68 fl oz/8 cups) soda base, add:

- seeds from 2 or 3 pomegranates or 1 tablespoon pomegranate molasses; 2 pieces orange peel; 1 vanilla pod; handful of rose petals; handful of fresh mint

- 1 kg (2 lb 3 oz) watermelon, flesh juiced; 2 tomatoes (juiced); 1 sliced lime; 125 ml (4 fl oz/½ cup) whey

- 1 chopped pear; 1 cup crushed red grapes; 3 cm (1½ in) piece fresh ginger, (unpeeled, chopped); 1 vanilla pod; 6 cardamom pods; 1 teaspoon black peppercorns; 2 star anise

- 1 chopped green apple; 2 chopped Lebanese (short) cucumbers; 1 sliced lime; ½ cup juniper berries; handful of mint

- 1 cup dried elderberries; 2 chopped plums; 1 vanilla pod; 1 star anise

- 5 organic dried or fresh figs, chopped; 2 dates (oil free); 2 cm (1 in) piece sliced ginger; 1 sliced lemon

- 1 chopped apple; 3–4 stems rhubarb, chopped; 2 cm (1 in) piece ginger (scrubbed, unpeeled and roughly chopped); 6 cardamom pods; 1 cinnamon stick; 1 vanilla pod

- 2 heads of elderflowers (remove as much twig as possible); 5 lemon slices

For any of the flavour combinations above, add all the ingredients to a jar with the soda base and stir well. Cover the jar with a cloth and stir a couple of times a day for 3 days. Then lid the drink. When the water is showing signs of fizz, open the jar and taste. Judge the flavour – if the liquid has soured somewhat and the flavour of the botanicals is evident, bottle it to encourage more fizz.

I strain out the fruit if it is spent but often leave in any herbs, spices or seeds. If the flavour needs a tiny boost, this is where you can add a bit more sugar or a squeeze of lemon juice, for example. Perhaps even a fresh sprig of something else for the bottle, or some flowers even. If you do this, then leave it for another 24 hours in the bottle on your bench before refrigeration. When your wild soda is really fizzy, you must refrigerate it. It will keep for a few weeks, but enjoy it within a just a couple of days of opening as the fizz will fade quickly once opened. If your brew has lost some fizz by being in the fridge, you can stimulate it a bit by adding a dash of sugar and letting it sit out on the bench for another day or two in its airtight bottle to coax it back.

NOTE: It's a good idea to use a plastic soda bottle until you work out how fizzy your brews get. You'll want to get used to the idea of gently and briefly burping your brews, or at least opening them with caution.

OTHER SODA IDEAS

YOGHURT SODA

This is a very simple way of making a fizzy drink – and it is fun for the kids. Add a couple of tablespoons of good, pot-set natural yoghurt to a 300–500 ml (10 fl oz–17 fl oz/2 cups) jar filled with fresh fruit juice, such as orange juice. Pop the lid on, shake it and sit it on the counter for a day or two – it will get lovely and fizzy just like that. Kind of like Orangina.

MILK KEFIR GRAIN SODA

Pop a teaspoon of spare milk kefir SCOBY (see page 134) straight into a 500 ml (17 fl oz/2 cups) bottle of organic fruit juice. Apple works well, as does grape: the grains will eat up the sugar. Shake well, and in a couple of days you'll come back to a fizzy, pleasantly sweet and living juice. The grains don't easily go back to milk from there, so make sure you have excess.

GROW YEAST

Prep. 15 minutes | Fermentation time: 1 week | Equipment: 100-500 ml
(3½-17 fl oz/2 cups) bottles, small balloons to fit the bottles

Growing yeast to start off your brew is a useful way to get to know the
chaotic yet symbiotic interaction between bacteria, yeast and sugar. Even
if you're not a brewer, you could do this purely for the fun of it, as an
experiment. For most wild sodas, you will simply rely on the fruit in the
ferment to start it, but some ferments require a strong and solid starter.
This is where you choose the type of starter – something that will work in
the substrate and not affect the flavour of the brew.

Here, we make two types of ferments for comparison: from variety of fruits
and existing yeasts from grains and from the sediment from a good craft
beer, mead or sake.

Try a couple of bottles from each category, or all of them if you have kids
around who are interested in this, too, to discover first-hand the different
strengths. Using a balloon on each of the bottles is not just a fun way to
see the release of carbon dioxide in your ferment, but it gives you a visual
indication of how active the yeast in each medium is. Sometimes I use
balloons on bottles purely to see what is happening, to note when it's very
active, or because we can't find an airlock or appropriate lid.

To catch and activate wild yeasts, you need fruit, vegetables or another
medium with yeast living on it, and sugars to feed those yeasts and coax

them to grow. Some things have both the sugar and yeasts – honey, apples, blueberries, raisins, plums, grapes and persimmons, for example. Things with a visible white bloom. Things that perhaps aren't so obvious are young pine cones, juniper berries, tomato leaves, wild flowers and seeds. Go ahead and trial some yourself to see how the yeast grows.

INGREDIENTS

```
water to fill each bottle, plus
  one fruit or grain option,
  plus a small amount of sugar
```

Fruit options

```
2 tablespoons raisins
400 g (14 oz) grapes
1-2 small apples
2-3 plums
1 tablespoon honey
sediment from a favourite brew,
  plus 1 teaspoon sugar
```

Grain options

```
1 tablespoon sourdough mother
  plus ½ teaspoon sugar
1 slice of raisin bread, broken
  into small pieces
3.5 g (¹⁄₁₀ oz/½ packet) bakers'
  yeast with a sprinkle of sugar
```

Make sure your hands, bottles and work area are clean. We don't want to introduce any surface yeasts into our experiment.

For the fruit ferments, blend or chop the fruit, then add to the bottle. Add the water and agitate to mix. Seal the bottle with a balloon or paper towel.

For the grain options, combine with the water and bottle as above.

Sit the bottles somewhere warm. Yeasts love 21°C (70°F), so keep that in mind when you choose a spot. Check on the bottles daily, agitating to mix the yeasts through. You should see the balloon slowly begin to fill after a couple of days – or not, depending on what you have chosen. Fizz in the liquid will be evident if you tap the bottle a little. Taste it to see what, if any, flavour there is. Some balloons will fill quickly, inflating the balloon so it's quite taut; others take much longer, only ever filling slightly.

When your yeast is fizzy and the balloon is filling, strain out any solids and use your experimental starter in a ferment. I regularly add a sourdough starter or ginger beer starter to my kvass (see page 42), or an apple yeast to give an apple cider a bit of a kickstart. If you have a good beer you like, grow yeast from that and add it to your beer instead of the packet yeast.

ROOT BEER

Prep. 15 minutes | Fermentation time: 5-10 days | Equipment: muslin (cheesecloth), 5 L (170 fl oz) jar or demijohn, airlock, bottles

I love the distinctive herbal flavours and aroma of homemade root beer and its earth-brown colour. Sassafras root beverages were made traditionally in North America for both culinary and medicinal reasons. Don't be daunted by the ingredients: they are easily sourced from health food stores and online. There is a tiny bit of wriggle room in the recipe – you could add or omit one or two things where you need to – but you *do* need the molasses, sassafras and sarsaparilla root.

Start the Ginger beer mother (page 130) 5 days ahead, if using.

INGREDIENTS

```
4 litres (135 fl oz/16 cups) water
1 vanilla pod
4 cinnamon sticks
2 star anise
1 tablespoon cacao nibs
1 teaspoon fenugreek seeds
2.5 cm (1 in) piece fresh ginger,
  chopped
½ cup birch bark
½ cup dried burdock root
½ cup dried sarsaparilla root
½ cup dried sassafras root
350 g (12½ oz/1 cup) molasses
raw sugar, to taste
approx. ½-1 cup ginger beer
  mother or brewer's yeast
  (see Note)
```

Bring the water to a boil in a saucepan over a high heat. Add all the other ingredients, excluding the sugar, ginger beer mother or yeast. Reduce the heat and simmer for 30 minutes. Take off the heat, and once cool enough to taste, do so. If you feel it needs to be sweeter, add some sugar to taste – I've deliberately kept the sweetener low in this recipe so you can add more, rather than reel back in regret. Keep in mind while tasting that it will sour slightly upon fermentation. Cool the brew to body temperature. Strain out the solids, then strain again through a cloth or coffee filter. Add the ginger beer mother or yeast and stir well.

Funnel into the jar or demijohn, lid with an airlock and set aside in a warm place for about 4 days. Gently agitate your brew every time you walk past, give it a little hello and see how it's coming along. It might take up to 10 days.

When ferment activity slows, siphon or pour it very carefully into clean bottles, avoiding the sediment at the bottom. Lid, label and refrigerate the bottles.

That lovely stuff at the bottom is flocculated yeast (yeast cells that have clumped together and fallen out of suspension after they ran out of work to do). You may want to keep that for your next brew as your yeast starter. Collect the yeast sediment, put it in a small jar with a teaspoon of sugar and a tablespoon of water, stir and cover with a cloth, and let it sit a day before closing and refrigerating.

NOTE: In this version I use a ginger beer mother, but you could use brewer's yeast (just follow the instructions on the packet) or a fruit yeast. Prepare the ginger bug ahead, doubling the recipe to yield one cup of liquid.

PEELING BIRCH BARK

BASQUE CIDER (SAGARDOA)

```
Prep. 2 hours | Fermentation time: 3 days, plus 7 days |
Equipment: juicer or fruit press, 5 L (170 fl oz) plastic tub,
muslin (cheesecloth), 2 demijohns with airlocks, siphon (optional),
bottles
```

Cider-making has long been part of the Basque Country's history, and the tradition of making it continues today: squashed apples, left out overnight, pressed again and then put in a barrel and opened a few months later. It has no added yeast or sugar, a light effervescence and low alcohol – usually around 2–3%.

A true Basque sagardoa relies on a mixture of sweet, tannic and sour apples – varieties traditionally planted in shared family plots. To replicate it with our own varieties, I use a mixture of regular sweet apples, sour green and crabapples with success, and these are fairly easy to find everywhere when in season.

Cider houses abound in the Basque region. There, they serve their sagardoa with meat-heavy foods, and it's pretty much a set menu that comes rolling out as you drink – chorizo, cod with green peppers, followed by steak, a Basque cheese, served with walnuts and quince. My brother says it's served in a 'this is what you're getting' way. You'll get your cider by placing your glass at a right-angle metres from the barrel and catching the cider as they pull out the txotx – the little stick blocking the opening.

With your own brew of Basque cider, the way to drink it is always in small portions – poured from a distance to aerate it and to create some bubbles just as you'd tip and roll a water kefir, a makgeolli or other old-style brews. You should only ever pour about 3 fingers deep each time, drink that and then refill. It's a bubble thing.

INGREDIENTS

```
6 kg (13 lb) organic apples
  (see Note)
approx. 200 g (7 oz/1 cup) soft
  brown sugar
```

Wash, dry and quarter the unpeeled apples, then press or juice the fruit into a large plastic tub: I use a masticating juicer, which does the job beautifully. For larger amounts, consider a fruit press; they can be hired. Leave the juice in the tub, covered with a cloth. Squeeze the pulp again, making sure to extract as much juice as possible; add this extra liquid to the juice tub.

Taste the juice. You may want to add sugar, depending on how tannic the apples are and how sweet the juice is – be guided by taste.

Cover the tub loosely with a cloth and leave it out for about 2 days. Stir it a couple of times a day, remembering to cover it between stirs to keep the vinegar bugs out. The apple juice needs this time to manifest the good bugs and create the right environment.

You will probably see some froth after a day or so, which is a good sign of fermentation. Depending on the temperature in the room, it may take a day or two longer. After 2–3 days of activity, the cider will be ready for the demijohns. Pour it through a cloth-lined strainer and funnel into the jars, leaving a bit of room at the top for movement. Then lid with a stopper and airlock. Leave it for another week to ferment, keeping an eye on it, taking some out with your wine thief (baster) to taste every couple of days. You don't want it getting too sour.

Rack into clean bottles, using a siphon (see page 32). You can pour it if you don't have a siphon, but tip it carefully to leave any yeasts on the bottom of the demijohn.

Refrigerate – or don't. There isn't a lot of sugar in this cider, so it should not be one of those explosive drinks. You might want to tip your bottle gently before opening, just to refizz a little.

When you serve your first bottle, remember to pour it from a great height and only a small measure. Pour some more and enjoy, with plenty of snacks, or try it with the fabulous Basque chicken cider recipe on page 200.

NOTES: I recommend a mixture of very fresh organic apples, sour, astringent and sweet – plenty of crabapples too. Keep in mind that 6 kg (13 lb) of apples usually reaps about 4 litres (135 fl oz) juice, which is about what we are after.

SAGARDOA

Sailors were known to prevent scurvy through the vitamin C content of sauerkraut in their diet, but in the Basque region, bordering Spain and France, it was all about the cider: it was more potable than water, so hundreds of barrels were stored away on ships for long voyages. The Basque language, culture and traditions suffered during the Francoist period in the drive to unite and homogenise Spain. However, the making of sagardoa was kept up in farms and villages, reemerging in the early 1970s.

Sagardoa is a living tradition in Basque Country, and it has extended into the etymology of place names and surnames: many start with sagar (apple) or other words relating to the pressing and fermenting of cider. I love the way it acknowledges those deep cultural roots.

This unwritten recipe comes from my sister-in-law Maitane. She is from San Sebastian, and this recipe has been passed down, just by word of mouth, through the generations. They have their own family orchard, full of different varieties of apples planted and cared for by their ancestors; they couldn't name the apples but there'll be cider in that orchard for everyone, for generations to come.

TEPACHE

Prep. 15 minutes | Fermentation time: 3-5 days | Equipment: 2 L
(68 fl oz) jar, muslin (cheesecloth), bottle

The surprising star of this spiced drink is pineapple – and not the flesh, but
the core and peel. It's a traditional low-alcohol drink in Mexico, sometimes
mixed with beer, served in clay mugs or sold at vendor stalls in bags
with straws.

Tepache is one of the easiest wild ferments to make because pineapple
contains a lot of natural sugars, which feed the yeasts that cohabit happily
within the crevices of the peel.

Serve ice cold on a hot day. If you were in Mexico, maybe you'd add a
splash of beer. It is also good in cocktails – I think anywhere you'd see lime,
tepache would be at home.

INGREDIENTS

```
1 organic pineapple
approx. 200 g (7 oz/1 cup)
  rapadura or brown sugar
  (see Note)
2 cloves
1 cinnamon stick
2 litres (68 fl oz/8 cups) water
```

With a sharp knife, peel and quarter the pineapple, removing the core.
Chop the peel and core into chunks and add to the jar with the sugar,
spices and water. Lid the jar and shake it vigorously to mix, then remove
the lid and cover loosely with a cloth.

Ferment for 3 days, then taste it. If it tastes tart and pineapple-y enough,
it is ready, but it may take a couple more days to develop that depth if the
surrounding temperature has been cool. Strain out the solids, then bottle.
Refrigerate.

*NOTE: In Central or South America, you'd use piloncillo or panela sugar, sometimes
shaped into a little cone. These are both similar to India's jaggery.*

Feed
and
grow

FEED AND GROW

CARE AND NURTURE

Growing botanicals, herbs and fungi yourself can be where the fermenter and the brew-witch meet. Having a bit of an apothecary garden always made sense to me for making food and for drinks – perhaps even more so for drinks, as you often need just a snip here and there. I believe the more variety in your garden or dried collections, the more interesting your drinks. But it's the magic in a jar on my bench that bewitches me the most. The process involved in fermenting makes me feel small (in a good way) and makes me wonder what else there is going on that we need to take more notice of. All that elemental biology at work is a great leveller.

In your fermenting life, you'll pick, snip, backslop, cut pieces of things, reinvent and reuse, buy, forage and grow, pour, (fail) and enjoy. As brewing and fermenting is intrinsically linked to beautiful, sometimes hard-to-find ingredients, I think it's reasonable to take your curiosity a bit further to the apothecary garden/ medicinal and culinary herb stage if you haven't already. The microbes fermenting in your jars and bottles will likely do better if the herbs and botanicals have come from rich soil just a few metres away. Your hands will like it too.

When you put a seed in the ground, or fungus spores on rice for kōji, wild yeast in a brew – you can't *make* them grow. Sometimes things don't work out as planned, and you'll have to stop, look and adjust a few things. The recipes in this chapter need feeding and caretaking so you can ferment with them. You'll nurture and feed and provide the right environment and then rely on their nature to do the work. That leaves the last ingredient, not listed but to keep your own outlook in place – *hope*. A little nod to nature.

MILK KEFIR JAR AFTER STRAINING

GINGER BEER MOTHER

Prep. 15 minutes | Fermentation time: 1-3 weeks | Equipment: 500 ml (17 fl oz/2 cups) jar, cloth

A ginger beer mother, also known as a ginger bug, is a starter made purely with ginger, sugar, water and time. You feed this every day until it starts to bubble and come alive – the same way you start a sourdough mother. This is an excellent and quite reliable starter to use as a boost for a Soda (pages 114–5), Black carrot kanji (page 100) or Beet kvass (page 99–100).

INGREDIENTS

2.5 cm (1 in) piece fresh ginger, unpeeled (plus an extra 5 pieces for feeding)
2 teaspoons raw sugar (plus extra for feeding)
250 ml (8½ fl oz/1 cup) unchlorinated water

Grate or finely chop the cleaned piece of ginger into the jar and add the sugar and water. Stir well. Cover with a piece of cloth, secure with a rubber band and place in a warm spot in your kitchen.

Every day, feed it the same amount of ginger and sugar, plus 2 tablespoons water. Stir well. The mix will start to bubble. After 5 days, your culture should be yeasty smelling and fresh; if so, it is ready to use as a starter culture.

Like a sourdough mother, you can keep a ginger bug in the fridge. Make sure to feed it the same menu once a week, leaving it out each time to warm up enough to start eating – a couple of hours is good – then put it back into the fridge.

Whenever you use any of the ginger beer mother, remember to replace whatever you took with the same quantity of fresh ingredients.

OTHER SODAS FROM A GINGER BEER MOTHER

Once your ginger bug is well established, strain off about 60 ml (2 fl oz/ ¼ cup) of the liquid and mix it into 1 litre (34 fl oz/4 cups) flavoured or infused water. You'll need sugar in there to feed the yeasts and get some happy fizz. Add about 10–50 ml (1–3 tablespoons) syrup of your choice, or a cup of chopped fruits and herbs, or just add the ginger mother to a green juice. Mix well, lid and let sit for 2–5 days. Ginger bug yeasts are very active and these drinks are infamous exploders: beware – bottling into plastic and prompt refrigeration is recommended.

WILD GINGER BEER

Prep. 30 minutes | Fermentation time: 4-10 days | Equipment: 2 L
(68 fl oz) jar, muslin (cheesecloth), bottles

INGREDIENTS

    400 g (14 oz) fresh ginger
    2 litres (68 fl oz/8 cups) water
    juice of 4 lemons
    approx. 125 ml (4 fl oz/½ cup)
      ginger beer mother, strained
      (see opposite)

Thinly slice the unpeeled ginger and put in a saucepan with the water and lemon juice. Bring to a simmer, allowing the flavours to infuse for about 20 minutes. Remove from the heat, add some honey and let cool.

Strain the mixture through a cloth into a jug and add the liquid from the ginger bug. Mix in well. Pour into bottles, lid and let ferment. Depending on the temperature, this could take anywhere from 4–10 days. This is a very fizzy brew so make sure to store it carefully, perhaps using plastic bottles or a balloon on top of one bottle to keep an eye on the carbonation level.

Once it's fizzy, pop the bottles into the fridge to slow down the ferment. It's important that you don't just leave the bottles out or they will fizz out and ruin. Refrigerate for a couple of days and enjoy. Always open with care.

A SCOBY BY ANY OTHER NAME

A ginger beer mother is an amazing and simple starter to make and use. However, the line-up of SCOBYs is a little different. I recommend you choose your SCOBY not just on the flavours or health benefits you'll get from the end product, but based on how much time you have to dedicate to it. SCOBY maintenance can be repetitive and can sometimes feel quite demanding and, for some people, even be guilt-inducing.

What is a SCOBY, and do you want one? A SCOBY is a Symbiotic Community/Colony of Bacteria and Yeast. It's held together in a polysaccharide matrix – a gel-like structure that is both fragile and strong. SCOBYs are often referred to as 'mothers' but go by many different names around the world. All of these mothers are beautiful, natural life forms. I'm often asked who makes them, or how to make them. The answer is: they are like a seed; they cannot be made, only grown. Comfortingly and fascinatingly, this kind of fermentation has existed alongside humans for a very long time, and when you get your first successful batch of milk or water kefir, jun or kombucha, you will probably wonder how the heck something so amazing could have been so absent from your life until now.

There are different SCOBYs that will make different drinks. Kombucha, jun and vinegar SCOBYs look like floating gel-like mushrooms that cover the surface of the liquid and also lurk at the bottom like stringy, yeasty sea creatures. Water kefir SCOBYs look like see-through, raw sugar crystals. Milk kefir SCOBYs are to me the most interesting. They are curled up like cauliflower and can be as wide as your palm when you flatten them out, depending on how they are fed. Both kefir SCOBYs are often called grains, although they are not grains at all. You need to get an initial amount of the kefir SCOBYs in order to make more; they will multiply once you start – I guess that's why they are called a mother.

Because all these SCOBYs are at their best when they have been fed and cared for, they really aren't something you can or should buy from a regular store. It's better to source them online from people who grow them specifically for sale, or from people who are fermenting at home already. The online space is great as there are plenty of maker groups out there with people willing to share. You can probably find one local to you. It's also possible to grow a kombucha SCOBY from the leftovers of an existing bottle of good, living, commercially made kombucha or jun. It's harder with the kefirs – unless a few tiny ones slipped through and are in the bottle. No harm in trying, but very unlikely. You can stretch out a milk kefir to make more milk kefir, but you usually won't be able to grow a SCOBY from this. Find one.

CHOOSE YOUR MOTHER

They all grow pretty easily and all make gorgeous drinks, so I'll just sum up the commitment level so you can make an educated decision. You'll have different energy, space and free time throughout your year and life, and I advise not to choose water kefir in those very busy, hectic or stressful times. (You probably won't listen …) Water kefir requires too much of you too often. Kombucha and jun, on the other hand, don't mind a bit of ignoring; they won't die if you leave them longer than you should, nor will they punish you for your neglect. No guilt at all. They are a good, forgiving, quiet and strong mother to have and to feed, and to keep and sometimes ignore on the shelf.

Kombucha

A kombucha SCOBY is a large pancake-shaped mother that feeds on tea and sugar. It prefers black tea, but you can fiddle around and use other teas successfully. Avoid teas that have essential oils; it won't matter too much but you can get an oily film on top of your drink if it's too strong. Kombucha is probably the most well-known of the 'soda' ferments and is readily available at supermarkets these days, although nowhere near as good as the kind you'll make yourself. I think the only way to buy really good kombucha is at a farmers' market if made by a small brewer.

Kombucha is a 7–14 day ferment, and it prefers a warm room. Depending on what you add, a 1–4 day second ferment in a bottle allows you to flavour it and can make it very fizzy.

Jun

Jun also has a large pancake-shaped mother, which is a bit lighter and brighter than kombucha. It's fed on green tea and honey. You can make other blends of tea for this too. It is as strong and resilient as kombucha. Jun has a minimum 3–5 day ferment at room temperature, is very mild and light and easy to flavour. You can mix your green teas with herbs, seeds and grasses for flavour and not have to add extra sugar in a second ferment. Depending on what you add, a second ferment in the bottle will take 1–3 days.

Water kefir

It has a 48-hour first ferment and a 24-hour second ferment. Its sparkle is strong, and it is so easy to flavour. It is the most like a regular soda because it comes from mostly lactic acid bacteria (rather than acetic acid, or vinegar, which drives kombucha). The demanding part of the schedule for water kefir is the continuous rotation. It also requires extra ingredients. Good water is important too, but unlike with the other brews, we're just using fresh water here, not boiling it and making tea. The SCOBY grows fast. You'll end up with quite a lot shortly into your journey.

Milk kefir

Milk kefir's mother feeds on the lactose in animal milk and can become very effervescent. It is very simple to make as all you need to do is pour milk over the SCOBY and let it sit for a day or two, agitating now and then if you think of it. It tastes like a drinking yoghurt only more complex and is known as the champagne of milk. There is a 24–48 hour first ferment, and an optional second ferment if you're after fizz or want more of the lactose to be eaten up and converted. Milk kefir is healthy, delicious, and in fact, my personal favourite. The thing to love about this is also the extensions – labneh, butter, whey soda – and you can take it backpacking or camping with you.

MILK KEFIR

In my experience, milk kefir has the potential to be the most effervescent ferment of them all. There is a tangy, fizzy, deep – almost goaty – flavour to milk kefir that you'll grow to love and crave. If you have restless sleeps or digestive issues, a shot before bed is so good, so restorative – milk kefir contains tryptophan (among many other amazing things), which is a relaxant. Milk kefir lines your gut and allows all the good bacteria to settle in and do their intended thing. Milk kefir adapts to go into seed, nut and oat milks too. It will just require a bit more stirring and may ferment faster.

Having milk kefir grains at hand is a great addition to your live culture collection. Not just for milk kefir. Use it strained to make a cheese, keep the whey to make soda or add the grains to a juice, which will make a sparkling (less sugar-laden) drink within days.

Milk kefir is a simple-to-make single-ferment drink. Its SCOBY needs to be fed milk of some kind; just as the other SCOBYs live off sugar, these guys live on the lactose in milk. Don't miss out on milk kefir because you don't normally consume milk; fermented milk becomes more digestible, low in lactose and has a longer shelf life. It can get fizzy and lively and is really very delicious.

Keep in mind that we've had our milk kefir tested and it came out at .9% alcohol. Not a lot – but if you add sugar for flavouring, you MUST leave it in the fridge. By adding sugar, you are feeding yeasts that will turn the sugar into a small amount of alcohol and a large amount of CO_2. Bottles can explode.

Milk kefir grains prefer cow's or goat's milk – even if you don't want to consume dairy you'll need to grow your grains and keep them going this way. You'll be able to pull the grains from a healthy dairy-fed batch to use them in something else. They'll usually work in a juice or a nut milk medium for five rotations until things start to go awry – they get out of balance, tired and need a rest. It's best to start again with fresh grains at that point. When you pull the grains out of the milk, just give them a rinse with your nut milk to get any dairy off.

Milk kefir usually contains more than 30 different strains of *Lactobacillus*, which makes it packed with probiotics and complexity. Remember, with all of these drinks it's not the amount of bacteria in your glass but the variety that is important.

Different to yoghurt, milk kefir ferments at room temperature, and where yoghurt is for eating, milk kefir is usually for drinking. That said, from milk kefir you can easily make kefir cultured butter, labneh and whey, soft and hard cheeses, yoghurt and dressings, or you can add it to smoothies, use it as a raising agent in pancakes and breads and even to marinate your meat. Anything buttermilk can do, milk kefir can do better. I just like to drink it straight up, but it is very easy to flavour.

Source your initial milk kefir grains from a fermenting friend or somewhere reputable online. There are powders that will make you about five batches, but they are not as potent as using the actual SCOBY.

THIS PAGE: MILK KEFIR SCOBY

NEXT PAGES: MILK KEFIR BREWING AND BEING STRAINED

MILK KEFIR

Prep. < 5 mins | Fermentation time: 24-48 hours | Equipment: 500 ml (17 fl oz) jar, muslin (cheesecloth), bottle

Fermenting fresh raw milk in the early days was done to extend its life. Not many of us have access to raw milk nowadays, but that's where the milk kefir SCOBY gets a gold star: when you ferment today's pasteurised milk with milk kefir grains, you are adding life to that milk – reversing the pasteurisation – *rewilding it* and keeping it drinkable for another month. It also could not be simpler.

INGREDIENTS

500 ml (17 fl oz/2 cups) milk
  (coconut, nut, oat, soy)
1 tablespoon milk kefir grains

Put the kefir grains into a jar. Add the milk – preferably not icy cold; let it sit on the bench for a bit before pouring over the grains. Cover with a lid or a cloth secured with a rubber band and leave it to sit on your bench for 24–48 hours at room temperature. I get the best, creamiest results when I stir it about twice a day. It will start to thicken, maybe separate and rise, so make sure there is room for that in the jar.

Strain with a fine strainer, then bottle and refrigerate the liquid. Keep the grains for another batch (see below). It should be thicker than milk, but still pourable, and smell lovely and fresh, sour – like Greek yoghurt. It will probably be slightly fizzy – that's my favourite thing! If not, set it out overnight on your bench and give it a gentle shake.

NOTES: You can make this a routine. Find out how much you'll drink and only make as much as that, as the grains prefer to remain in regular use rather than making large batches and then putting them to rest. The grains should grow and become quite plentiful. Don't throw them out – share them around or save some for another time. Be warned – you can lose them along the way: they can shrink, or even disappear, particularly in the winter. So keep some spare. It's also great to have some spare for other experi-ferments.

To store the grains, cover them with some milk and put them in the fridge for a month, refreshing the milk now and then. For longer breaks, dry them out between two paper towels and sprinkle them with a bit of milk powder, then put them back into a jar and into your freezer. They will keep for months like that but will take a fair bit of convincing to wake up – maybe 2 or 3 rotations.

There are plenty of myths about never using metal with milk kefir. We ferment the milk kefir in high-grade stainless steel at The Fermentary, and I've always used a metal strainer. Just make sure you use non-reactive metals, such as stainless steel, and don't scrape metal on metal – be gentle. Plastic is okay too.

FURTHER IDEAS

– Kefir freezes well and the beneficial bacteria survive too. Pouring your kefir into an ice-cube tray is handy to add to smoothies.

– Blitz any frozen fruit and some milk kefir in a blender for a quick and nutritious smoothie. Try freezing these blends into icy poles. Kids love them – and they are a great way to get good bacteria into a gut. I've been known to serve them for breakfast.

– Pop a teaspoon of jam into your milk kefir if you're in a hurry.

– Flavour milk kefir with syrups (see pages 178–81). Our latest favourite is Earl Grey tea syrup: stir into the milk kefir and let it steep in the fridge overnight.

– Masala chai is also wonderful, as is a blend of black sesame, coconut sugar, cinnamon and vanilla.

WHEY FOR A SODA

Once you have a thick milk kefir, pour it into a lined sieve, put over a bowl and leave it to drain overnight. The strainer will hold the milk – now labneh – and the bowl will hold a lovely and powerful whey. Keep the whey in a bottle in the fridge or freeze into ice cubes to use – this is awesome stuff. Use this for Whey soda or Wild soda (pages 112–15).

TAKE A TRAVELLER

I guess a nomadic lifestyle is where we all came from, and milk kefir suits this. Because milk kefir is mesophilic, meaning it ferments at room temperature, this is a wonderful culture to take travelling with you. My parents, like many, take their caravan on the road every year or go on cruises, and this is like a little tummy insurance for them.

Milk kefir even loves UHT long-life milk as there is no competition – it goes straight to the lactose and eats it all up. It is a great way to line your gut when you might be a bit vulnerable away from your usual food sources and kitchen routine.

A little travellers kit for milk kefir

Pack a tablespoon of grains into a little jar, perhaps a 500 ml (17 fl oz/ 2 cups) jar, then secure it in a waterproof packet such as a resealable bag. No matter where you are you can usually find those tetra packs of milk in the supermarket or bar fridge. When you arrive at your destination, pour the milk into the jar and let it sit. A day or two later, it will be ready to drink straight or be strained into a glass. Hang on to the grains and start again – by this time, you'll have worked out where to get some more milk.

WATER KEFIR

Kefir, in Turkish, means joy, or pleasure. Water kefir has a few names, depending on who gave the gelatinous 'grains' to you or where you live. You'll see it called tibicos, snow lotus, water crystals or water babies. Water kefir grains are jelly-like cells thought to come from an aloe plant of some kind, but others say they come from a ginger beer mother, and yet others think they are from within a water lily plant. Really, the origins are unknown and these days you're going to get them simply from someone who has some. Whether through a friend, in a store or online – the first thing to do is to source some grains.

Kefir is a culture that relies on this kind of sharing for survival – it doesn't have death planned into its natural life, but other than the drink it makes, and being able to grow prolifically, it doesn't have a natural way of spreading itself around without help from us. Unlike kombucha, where you can grow another mother just from a good brew – or even from the bottle you bought at the store – you can't grow water kefir SCOBYs. Water kefir also requires a little more attention than kombucha and jun or even wild sodas, mostly because it brews fast and needs more feeding and care because of that.

Milk and water kefir have some similarities. They are both rich in a wide array of *Lactobacillus* and yeast strains, are a comparatively quick ferment, and prefer to be free and able to travel up and down the jar as they like. You could use water kefir grains in milk and vice versa, but only for small periods of time. Milk kefir grains are more at home in milk, eating the lactose, while water kefir grains need simple sugar and water as their main diet. As you feed them, and when they're happy, they will procreate like crazy and you'll either share them with friends, make larger batches or dispose of them in your compost. See page 147 for how to save water kefir grains for later.

Some people develop cravings for water kefir and worry that they are drinking too much of it. This infatuation and craving period usually lasts about 3–6 weeks before it balances out, so don't worry about it too much. So, how much *should* you drink? Everything in moderation of course, but if you have a delicate digestive system or think you may not tolerate living foods like this, start off slowly and increase incrementally until you are just enjoying it like a regular soda. We have a bottle of it at the dinner table most nights.

I'll pat myself on the back and tell you that we have won awards with this very recipe, have sold thousands and thousands of bottles of it and taught just as many people. There are two stages to this ferment: the first ferment is to feed the grains and wake up the yeasts; the second ferment is to flavour the kefir. But this is just the bouncing-off point – get creative, get to know your grains with your available ingredients, and enjoy the amazing flavours you can get from the second ferment.

STRAINING WATER KEFIR

WATER KEFIR: FIRST FERMENT

Prep. up to 20 minutes | Fermentation time: 48 hours | Equipment:
3 L (101 fl oz) jar with lid, bottles (at second ferment)

INGREDIENTS

1 cup water kefir grains
110 g (4 oz/½ cup) organic raw
  (demerara) sugar (see Notes)
pinch of bicarbonate of soda
  (baking soda) or salt
¼ teaspoon molasses
1 slice ginger, washed well and
  unpeeled
1 organic lemon, halved
dried organic fruit (I recommend
  1 date and 1 fig - see Notes)
2 litres (68 fl oz/8 cups) water
  (preferably filtered, rain or
  spring)

Combine all the ingredients, except for the water, in a clean jar. Add the
water and give it all a gentle stir with a wooden spoon. Secure with an
airtight lid – kefir likes an anaerobic environment. However, it will do fine if
you prefer to ferment aerobically – there'll be marginally less effervescence
and less alcohol that way.

Water kefir prefers a fairly consistent temperature of about 18–22°C
(64–72°F). Keep your kefir in a spot that's most likely to remain at that
temperature and leave it for 48 hours, stirring or agitating now and then.
For the sole purpose of watching something else work while I toil at my
computer, I like to put my jar where I can see it. You'll notice some action:
the grains travelling up the jar, little explosions in the bottom sending
bubbles up.

After 48 hours, strain your water kefir into a jug or bowl through a fine
strainer, making sure to catch all the grains. Discard the ginger and fruit and
put the grains back into a jar to make another batch. Keep the kefir liquor
until you are ready for the second ferment (see page 144).

*NOTES: You can experiment with coconut sugar or other natural sweeteners. If you
use a darker sugar such as rapadura, you won't also need the molasses. I don't
recommend using raw honey – the bacteria can affect the kefir grains. Any dried
fruit (or citrus) you use should be unwaxed and not coated in oils or sulphates. Use
sultanas (golden raisins) to feed the water kefir if you don't have a fig or a date.*

*Omit the ginger and molasses in the first ferment if you are planning to make a very
delicate or subtle flavouring in the second ferment, such as rose petals. It's also good
to omit the molasses at this stage when you are hoping for a clearer brew. See page
152–4 for flavouring ideas.*

The first ferment period is mostly about feeding the grains. They'll eat the sugars, benefit from the other ingredients and also have some influence on the flavours you want. Mostly, this is where the lactic acid bacteria sour the water to make the yeast comfortable enough to help eat more sugar and create more carbon dioxide. It doesn't get so sour that they die – they live in perfect harmony together until the day they are ignored. When that happens, it really can get too sour and you lose the balance. Try not to do that.

This recipe provides the water kefir SCOBYs with all their nutritional requirements. They will produce a gorgeous drink – but please know that this certainly isn't the only way to make them happy. It depends on the kind of water you have as well as the environment they are in – there may be times where you need to fiddle around and put less iron- and mineral-rich ingredients in, and every now and then you may need to give your grains a break by just feeding them sugar, ginger and lemons, for example. Feel free to omit parts of the recipe here and there as you like. As long as there is water and a form of sugar, they will live. If they start to look ill or disappear, you should get back to the full recipe and give them some love.

WATER KEFIR GRAINS AND LEMON SLICES
IN A WOVEN STRAINER

WATER KEFIR: SECOND FERMENT

The second ferment takes 24 hours. It's where the art lies. It's a really lovely way to experiment with complex flavours – herbs, spices, fruit or vegetables. It could be as simple as a handful of frozen berries, the juice of a lemon, a few slices of ginger, or you can pop in a cinnamon stick or vanilla pod. It's easy to add another slice of lemon and ginger and a dried fig and let it steep in the bottle, leaving it there even when serving. Or you could make syrups and juices and use those. This is the fun part.

It's also when the natural carbonation occurs. Some warnings: just like for any other living drink, you need to use a thick, very good-quality bottle for this and only leave it out for 24 hours or less because it will keep fermenting when at room temperature. If you add too much sugar/sweet fruit, the kefir will also become more alcoholic and carbonated with time. Kefir can honestly become explosive. It's much better to put it in the fridge for the second ferment than risk it by leaving it out for longer. A 12-hour second ferment is fine too.

The second ferment steps are simple. After you've strained out the grains, pour the liquid into clean bottles. Add the flavourings and lid. Sit the bottles in an upright position, out of the way – even better in an esky or something that will protect you from any explosions – and wait.

NOTES: Remember not to sterilise your equipment with anything too strong that leaves a residue as this could kill your bacteria. A hot dishwasher or citric acid is perfect.

There are so many little things you'll pick up once you get into your water kefir routine, and you'll find ways to troubleshoot problems as you go. Sometimes your culture will go slimy, reduce in size, stop growing, not make a fizzy brew, smell sulphuric. Usually you need to break apart your method as there are so many variables. What is in the water? Is it iron-rich? Cut back on the ingredients that are rich in those things, such as the date and molasses. Sometimes, the grains stop in cold weather and they need to be put in a warmer place to become active again. Sometimes I put them out in the sun for warmth and for a bit of UV, which they seem to love. Try to omit ingredients that have seeds so you don't have seeds going through your grains, and watch out for paper from the dates. Sometimes just giving your grains a dose of fresh ginger, white sugar and a lot of lemon will help balance things out. Connect the dots and pare it down, then build it back up again.

Over the next 24 hours, your kefir will take on some colour (depending on what you put in there) and become flavoured and fizzy. If that doesn't happen, perhaps you needed more of the flavour – or maybe the drink needs a bit more time. This is not an exact science, but you can get it pretty close. I think 10 ml (¼ fl oz/about ½ tablespoon) freshly juiced ginger per litre (34 fl oz/4 cups) is the right amount, plus the same quantity of pomegranate molasses. I have several large syringes for syrups and juices made up; I just bottle the drinks plain, then squirt those syrups in as needed.

TONIC WATER KEFIR

Make 2 litres (68 fl oz/8 cups) of the base water kefir recipe (page 142), with a couple of tweaks. Omit the molasses and ginger and add a 125 ml (4 fl oz/ ½ cup) lemon juice and the peel of 2 lemons. This is because we want a fairly clear tonic, and the molasses will taint it somewhat.

For the second ferment, if you don't like or have lavender, leave it out. In fact, the most important ingredients here are the cinchona bark, lemon, lime and orange and perhaps the extra sugar. The others are luxuries.

INGREDIENTS

```
15 g (½ oz) cinchona bark
juice of 1 lime
juice of ½ orange
2 stalks lemongrass
2 allspice berries
3 green cardamom pods
1 sprig lavender
¼ teaspoon salt
2 tablespoons sugar (to taste)
```

Combine all the ingredients in your jar or divide into bottles. Pour water kefir in, lid and agitate by giving it all a good yet gentle shake: we aren't making cultured butter here – we are shaking it more like an expensive snow globe. Treat it like that – it is rather beautiful, so leave it out to ferment somewhere you will see it and can gently agitate it as you walk by. Your tonic will be ready and should be fizzy within 24–48 hours. If not, keep it out a bit longer. Refrigerate and enjoy. (See page 179 for Tonic syrup.)

ELDERFLOWER WATER KEFIR

Pretty and delicate elderflower makes a beautiful flavouring in water kefir. First, make 2 litres (68 fl oz/8 cups) water kefir (page 142), without molasses or ginger, and use 2 whole lemons, sliced.

For the second ferment, strain out the water kefir grains, put the liquid back into the jar, and put the lemon slices back. Add 50 elderflower stalks, 2 sliced oranges and 220 g (8 oz/1 cup) sugar.

Close the lid and let sit for 3 days in the fridge. Then strain off the solids, taste, add sugar if needed and bottle. If there is no carbonation, let it sit in the bottle another day until there is.

ROSE, CARDAMOM AND VANILLA WATER KEFIR SECOND FERMENT

We make a beautiful water kefir out of the gorgeous rose petals from Acre of Roses near The Fermentary. Sometimes, the brew is a dark, deep red, other times it is a lighter yellow, depending on the colour of the petals that day. The Mr Lincoln rose starts off pink and slowly deepens in the bottle to a purple and then dark blue. It's very subtle and a bit musky.

Make 2 litres (68 fl oz/8 cups) light first ferment water kefir (as for the Elderflower recipe, page 145). Strain, then add a tightly packed cup of chemical-free rose petals, 5 cracked cardamom pods and a vanilla pod.

If you feel it needs sweetening, add 55 g (2 oz/¼ cup) sugar. Ferment in the jar, with the lid on, for about 24 hours. Once the colour has changed and the bubbles are visible, strain and bottle, perhaps putting a couple more cardamom pods in. This is also a delicious way to flavour milk kefir.

PRICKLY PEAR WATER KEFIR

We've made prickly pear-flavoured water kefir most years, much to the disdain of our staff. They are, as the name suggests, really quite prickly! However, the water kefir is almost fluorescent and so delicious that it's worth the spikes. You only need 1–2 pieces of fruit per litre.

Make your first ferment of water kefir (page 142) with lime instead of lemon and, if available, substitute 1 litre (34 fl oz/4 cups) of the plain water with aloe juice. At the second ferment, take the skins off the prickly pear (wear gloves). Chop the fruit and simply add to the jar, mashing the fruit as you add it. Add a few pieces of lime as well. Pour over the first ferment water kefir, sealing the bottle. Let it sit for 24 hours.

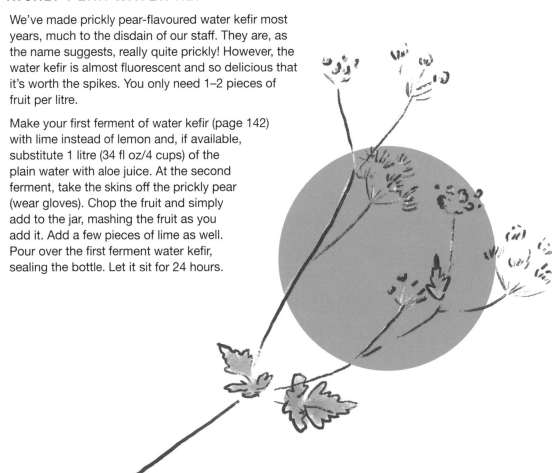

STORING WATER KEFIR SCOBY

Water kefir SCOBYs are like functional sea monkeys. Your very own quite demanding pets that will provide you with not only a probiotic powerhouse, a delicious carbonated drink, a very cool mixer, but also with something amazing to talk and think about.

At worst, though, they can become a nagging pain, reminding you that you have work to do, something to feed … no sugar in the cupboard … no empty bottles.

Water kefir grains will live forever if you look after them well. But that's a lot of work. You'll need a rest at some point, and you'll also want to share them with people.

Most people enjoy an era of it, a season of water kefir, usually in the summer each year. If you want to then suspend operations, you can either freeze or dehydrate the grains, waking them up to use when you are in the mood again. Both are easy methods and will ensure you have grains when the craving and the time to ferment again returns.

To freeze: Spread water kefir grains out in a single layer on paper towel, cover with paper towel and let dry overnight. Pop into a container, sprinkle with some raw sugar, then seal the jar and freeze. To defrost, just pull them out, and as soon as they are thawed, put them into a small jar with water and the ingredients for a brew. The first brew may not work; it may take 2-3 rotations before they'll come alive again.

To dehydrate: Spread water kefir grains in a single layer in your dehydrator and dry for at least 24 hours at 36°C (97°F). It may take a bit longer - check them. They will shrink; you don't want them too small, but you want to make sure there isn't any water available. When they are dry, put them in an envelope or something else breathable for another day or so, then put them in a jar. They'll keep like that for a long time. This is a great way to gift your grains.

To wake up: Empty your container of water kefir grains into a jar of 750 ml-1 litre (25½-34 fl oz/3-4 cups) water (preferably living water - filtered or rain; avoid chlorinated water), add about 55 g (2 oz/¼ cup) organic raw sugar and stir gently. Pop a lid on your jar and leave for 4-7 days to rehydrate and wake up. After this time, the grains should be all plump and look alive and even bounce in your hand. If they don't, and the water is still quite sweet, you may need to sit them out a bit longer somewhere warmer and give them a bit of a stir now and then. They'll wake up - they may just need some nurturing.

KOMBUCHA AND JUN

Kombucha is a mainstream drink that is now found in all supermarket fridges (and shelves!), a relatively new development in the drinks industry. If you aren't familiar with it, I'm glad to be the one to introduce it to you.

Kombucha and jun are both tea vinegar sodas. When you make either kombucha or jun yourself, it will be a living, naturally sparkling, mildly acidic and really refreshing drink with a very small amount of residual alcohol.

Before you can start, you need to get hold of a good-quality bottle of kombucha or jun, or you need to source a SCOBY. They are now easier to find than ever: through word of mouth, at a market or through a trusted online source. Aim for a SCOBY that isn't refrigerated, which is not a good place for it to be (nor will you know for how long it has been refrigerated). Look for an online seller who tells you how they look after it, and who can be contacted afterwards for help if needed, rather than buying a kit in the store – particularly if that kit is in the fridge.

You're going to need not just the SCOBY itself, but about 250 ml (8½ fl oz/ 1 cup) of the SCOBY liquid. You'll add your sweet tea to this base, cover it with a cloth to keep bugs and the rest of the world out, and let it sit and ferment in a warm environment. Once your SCOBY is fed and in the jar, it may need time to settle in for the first brew. A thin film should form within a week. This is your new mother. Try and let it be, to grow further without disturbing it until the SCOBY is confidently sitting atop the liquid.

In the fermenting process, the sugars will get consumed and converted to both acetic acid, lactic acid bacteria, alcohol and carbon dioxide. When the liquid is mildly effervescent and tastes sour, you'll strain out most of the liquid (remembering to always leave at least 80 ml/2½ fl oz/⅓ cup to start the next batch with) and bottle it, adding herbs or fruit for flavour. Lid the bottle and let it sit at room temperature for a few days while it carbonates.

There are two common ways of brewing at home: batch brewing and continuous brew. I suggest you start with small batches before scaling up. See page 155 for more on the continuous method.

What I love about kombucha and jun is that you can make a really good tea mix and not need to second ferment with fruits. For a herbal tea lover, this adds a layer – no longer just hot or cold, you now have sparkling and fermented. Getting a younger person to drink oat straw or tulsi tea can be hard work, but not disguised as a soda.

KOMBUCHA AND JUN
FIRST FERMENT

Prep. 10 minutes | Fermentation time: 4-14 days | Equipment: 2-3 L
(68-101 fl oz) wide-mouthed jar, muslin (cheesecloth), bottles

Jun and kombucha are practically the same thing – with a couple of small
differences. Jun tea ferments quicker, prefers green tea and honey, and lives
well in a cooler environment. It's a milder brew and lighter flavoured; the
mother is also lighter and more porous, which is somehow more appealing
and charming (to me). Kombucha is made with black tea and sugar.

INGREDIENTS

Kombucha

2 tablespoons black tea or 3 tea bags
1 litre (34 fl oz/4 cups) boiling water
75 g (2¾ oz/⅓ cup) sugar
1 kombucha mother with 125 ml (4 fl oz/
  ½ cup) already brewed kombucha

Jun

2 tablespoons green tea or 3 tea bags
1 litre (34 fl oz/4 cups) boiling water
115 g (4 oz/⅓ cup) organic raw honey
1 jun mother with 125 ml (4 fl oz/
  ½ cup) already brewed jun tea

Brew your tea with very hot water, and once the water has cooled slightly,
mix in the sugar or honey and stir to dissolve. When the sweet tea cools
to body temperature, add it to your jar, then add the already brewed
kombucha or jun and then the mother. Cover the jar with cloth or paper
towel and secure with a rubber band. Set aside in a nice warm spot, ideally
24°C (75°F), and in a place with fresh air, but not in direct sunlight. It's nice
to have it nearby, somewhere you'll be able to see it changing and brewing.

Your brew should ferment within 3–7 days. Taste it to see if it's soured at all.
Sometimes it takes a bit longer and sometimes it happens sooner. If you
want to speed it up, just add more 'pre brew' to it. When it's sour with a hint
of effervescence, bottle it, (remembering to keep some for your next batch)
and add your preferred second ferment ingredients, then let it sit another
day or two until lightly carbonated.

NOTES: If your brew over-ferments and becomes too acidic, keep it for vinegar, use it as a vinegar in Fire tonic (page 173), or to make mustard. If you get tired of brewing, don't put your SCOBY in the fridge – this will damage some of the yeasts and can cause mould. Sit it aside in a dark place and let the mothers grow (see page 158–9). When you are ready to brew, peel off a layer (not the top one) and start again.

As with all brews, it's important to keep your work area, hands, vessels and equipment clean and don't use harsh detergents. Hot water works well.

Use your best water to brew the tea (see Notes on water on page 18).

ON BREWING TEA FOR KOMBUCHA AND JUN

Possibly the world's most popular infusion, tea is mostly brewed as a staple daily beverage, but many tea varieties make a great base for other drinks. Pu'erh, for example, has a very interesting profile. It goes well with cola and root beer flavours (pages 118-19), and can be used in your kombucha or jun base. Pu'erh also adds a beautiful earthy and deep base to a shrub (pages 171-2) or when thrown into a mead, or you can add some flecks of it into a second ferment water kefir (pages 144-6). Pu'erh tea improves with age. It is fermented, and often stored and sold in a compressed cake or brick form. The stages in preparing the pu'erh tea go something like this: break the cake, wake it by letting it breathe and then brew. This tea has a refreshing, almost enlivening property - the flavours vary from chocolate hints to stone fruits, musky soil, dark wine, mushrooms, smoky whiskey to wet tatami (my own special tasting note). For fermenting and flavouring, pinch some leaves from the cake, add them to the brew and strain them out later.

If you want to blend herbs with your tea, keep the traditional green or black at 50%, and if you want to push it further, build on it over a few batches to get to 30% tea and 70% herbal mixture, keeping an eye on the health of your SCOBY.

And here's a tip for bigger brews. If I'm making a 4 litre (135 fl oz/16 cups) batch, quite often I will brew 1 litre (34 fl oz/4 cups) boiling water with the sugar (or honey) until it's dissolved, then add the tea and steep for longer - maybe 10 minutes. In the meantime, I pour the remaining water into my vessel and then add the hot tea 'concentrate' without needing it to cool down, as the water will do that for me. The mixed water temperature is perfect then - warm - so I add the actual jun or kombucha pre-brew, then the mother and cover the vessel. This makes it easier than brewing 4 litres (135 fl oz/16 cups) of hot tea and cooling it all.

SECOND FERMENT IDEAS
FOR WATER KEFIR, KOMBUCHA AND JUN

After your brews are finished with their first ferment, you'll strain off the grains or mother and ready your jars for another brew. You'll bottle your drink and wait for the carbonation. But first – flavour!

This is the exciting part. The foraging and creative ideas play out without too much risk as you are usually only doing a 1 litre (34 fl oz/4 cups) bottle. If it doesn't work, you can add more, or know better for next time.

These are purely suggestions and something to help you on your way. Do not hold back if you want to add more or less, change the combinations or make up your own imagined flavours the first time. Go for it. Kefir in particular will suck the colour out of anything and turn that hue within a day. It's fabulous to watch.

The sugar at this point will convert to alcohol, which rarely reaches more than 2.5%, but it is something you need to consider depending on who is drinking it. Simple high sugar additions, such apple juice, will yield something different and less sophisticated than adding a few pieces of apple into the kefir with a cinnamon stick, for example.

TIP: When you are using fresh fruit, if you have time (particularly for softer fruit), freezing it first and defrosting before adding it to your kefir will enhance the flavour.

The suggestions below are for 1 litre (34 fl oz/4 cups) water kefir, kombucha or jun. Bottle the brew into your vessel, add the flavours, lid and sit for a further 24 hours for water kefir, and between 2–5 days for jun and kombucha. Refrigerate. If, for some reason, the brew is still quite sweet and isn't fizzy yet, leave it for another day, keeping an eye on it and gently agitating it to move the flavours and yeast around. Have a strainer ready to strain as you pour.

- 2 dried apricots; small twig of thyme

- 1 tablespoon fresh raspberries; ½ lime, squeezed and dropped in

- 2 tablespoons strawberries; 10 cracked black peppercorns

- 5 green coffee beans; elderberry syrup to taste (about 1 tablespoon)

- handful of smashed cherries; small piece of vanilla pod; 1 star anise

- long piece of papaya, fresh or dried; schisandra berries; a few pounded cacao nibs; use in coconut water kefir or regular kefir

- ¼ cup dried strawberry gum leaves or tea; 1 finger lime, cut in half

STRAINING THE SECOND FERMENT

- couple of slivers of watermelon; handful of fresh basil
- ½ cup chopped rhubarb; a few pieces of apple; pinch of green tea
- ½ cup chopped rhubarb; 1 tablespoon coffee beans
- 1 cucumber, chopped; small handful of mint; ½ lime, sliced and wedges squeezed in
- smoky oolong tea; fermented lavender honey
- ½ cup violets; 5 bashed green fennel seeds
- coffee (for kombucha/jun, swap out one cup of the tea and add a strong cup of coffee); vanilla bean
- 5–10 whole hop flowers; ¼ cup grapefruit juice or 3–4 dried apricots
- couple of slices of peach; 2 blackberries; 2 sage leaves

PLAY WITH THE TEA AND FLAVOUR

With kombucha and jun, I'm passionate about making the tea shine as much as any second ferment flavours. Here are some of my favourite teas plus flavours to add at second ferment. Don't forget, you can play around with tea alone and not worry about the fruit or sweeteners at all. It may not get as fiercely carbonated as it does when you add something sweet, but this style is really well suited for a continuous brew situation (see opposite page).

FOR KOMBUCHA
- Earl Grey; sugar; blackberries
- rooibos; sugar; 2–3 apricots; 1 tablespoon dried angelica
- pu'erh; sugar; 2 prunes

FOR JUN
- genmaicha; brown rice syrup
- green rooibos; honey; pine needles; juniper berries; lemon
- rooibos; honey; cinnamon
- green tea, tulsi, oat straw; honey; dried white mulberries; rosemary sprig; pinch of dried lavender
- green tea, oat straw; honey; raspberries

CONTINUOUS BREW

This is absolutely the most convenient and lifestyle-friendly way to brew, saving time and clean up, allowing you to take as much as you want, when you want. You can tap out the kombucha or jun for second fermentation, or simply tap out a glass to enjoy straight from the barrel. I like to keep a small cup nearby for tasting the brew each morning, to see where it's at.

If you can get hold of the right kind of crock for this, then I recommend you do. Just using one of those glass jars you get for parties or a regular tapped vessel for drinking water is not ideal. The mother in these brews is messy, things sink to the bottom and get caught in the tap. Slime blocks the tap. You need a vessel that has been designed for this and has a high enough tap to allow the 'sludge' to sink down to the bottom. It should also be big enough to hold at least 5-7 litres (170-235 fl oz).

Make your first brew as you would a batch brew, and when that is ready you simply remove 75% of it through the tap or spigot into bottles to second ferment. The remainder is your 'starter brew'. With the correct vessel, the right amount will be calculated to sit under the tap so there is no danger of taking too much.

Add your cooled sweet tea to the vessel, gently pulling aside the mother as you pour, cover and wait. As there is a fair amount of active yeast and more fermented tea in the bottom of the vessel than with a batch brew, it will ferment faster: it will be ready within 2-7 days.

If you are running a cafe or restaurant and want to keep a brew constant, this would mean finding your own rhythm, perhaps even having the tea ready every day or two depending on your needs, topping it up each night. If you are only adding small amounts at a time, then it will be ready overnight, and you'll always have your kombucha or jun tea ready to pull.

REMINDERS AND TIPS

- At second ferment, your drinks can get very fizzy, which is why you don't want to leave them out for too long lest you have an explosion. Use plastic bottles, or put glass bottles in a protected spot.

- The more sugar involved, the more alcohol you'll produce - ingredients such as apple juice will certainly make a ferment stronger. Our average ABV for real water kefir is 1-2% on a small amount of dried fruit.

- A reminder to be clean all the time (hands and surfaces and containers), yet don't be too heavy-handed with your sanitising. You want clean jars, but don't use heavy bleaches, which may leave residue that would kill your bacteria. Boiling water is enough for sterilising in this case. Or even just using the dishwasher, if you have one.

- Water kefir can become very powerful - enough to break jars - so avoid square or flimsy cheaper jars and go for good-quality thick glass.

- If you can't be back after 48 hours or in time to take kefir out for a second ferment, cover the jar with a cloth and rubber band rather than a lid and attend to it when you get back.

- If you are away for more than a week, think about freezing or dehydrating your grains.

- Kefir grains can change, and they can sometimes be quite difficult to get back into action. Corrective action may be required: separate them into smaller jars and simplify the recipe, reducing the variables.

SMOKY COLA KOMBUCHA

Prep. 30 minutes | Fermentation time: 7-14 days, plus 4-7 days |
Equipment: 5 L (170 fl oz) jar, muslin (cheesecloth), bottles

INGREDIENTS

4 litres (135 fl oz/16 cups) water
3-5 tablespoons pu'erh tea (see
  page 151)
220 g (8 oz/1 cup) sugar
250 ml (8½ fl oz/1 cup) already-
  made kombucha

At second ferment

juice and zest of 3 lemons
juice and zest of 4 limes
15 dried sour cherries
2 prunes
6 large cinnamon sticks
2 tablespoons coriander seeds,
  bashed
1 tablespoon grated nutmeg
2 vanilla beans, split
1 star anise

Brew the pu'erh tea, then prepare the pu'erh kombucha in your fermenting jar following the base method on page 150. Brew for 7-14 days depending on the temperature and on how active your brew is.

When ready, add the second ferment flavourings and leave the brew to steep for a further 4-7 days with the lid on. Taste after 4 days to see how it's getting on – perhaps add some more sugar if needed.

Strain and bottle. If there is no effervescence yet, leave it on the counter for another couple of days – keeping an eye out for pressure building in the bottles – or just refrigerate and let steep cold.

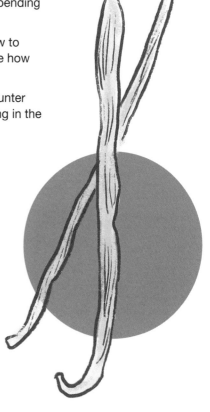

TOASTY TEA KOMBUCHA

Prep. 20 minutes | Fermentation time: 3-7 days | Equipment: 2 L
(68 fl oz) jar, muslin (cheesecloth), bottles

INGREDIENTS

2 litres (68 fl oz/8 cups) mugicha
or other roasted grain tea
1 tablespoon lapsang souchong tea
(oolong or another smoky tea
would do)
1 tablespoon blackstrap molasses
or Date syrup (page 179)
4 tablespoons sugar
125 ml (4 fl oz/½ cup) already-
made kombucha
1 small kombucha mother

At second ferment

2 pink peppercorns
3-5 crushed coriander seeds

While the mugicha tea is still warm, add the lapsang tea leaves and let
brew to the strength you like. Strain into your fermenting jar and add the
molasses or date syrup, if using. Remember, you can add more but you
can't take it out, so go slowly. Add the sugar.

When the brew has cooled down to body temperature, add the made
kombucha and the mother. Say something nice, cover the vessel with cloth
and secure with a rubber band. It will be quite quick to brew – check every
couple of days.

When it's ready, bottle it (remembering to leave enough behind for your
next brew), adding the peppercorns and coriander seeds. Lid and sit on the
bench for a couple of days checking for fizz. Refrigerate.

SCOBY NOTES

KOMBUCHA AND JUN

To store
Unlike our water kefir friends, who will just slowly disappear if you ignore them, the kombucha and jun mothers are happy to remain, suspended in time for extended periods. Months even. When it's time to brew again, just pull off the top layer, choose a freshie and start again. As you brew more, you'll also gather new baby's each time. You can take them off if it is getting too thick and store them in a jar with tea, in a kind of hotel. Whether storing or making a hotel for spare mothers, make a batch of kombucha, cover as normal and let sit somewhere out of the way but as per the normal recipe, a place where there is fresh air. The SCOBYs will grow, one on top of the other, until the jar is full of layers of kombucha mothers.

To share
It's good to be able to give your friends your SCOBYs. Try and give a nice thick one – not a brand new thin layer, but not too thick either. One that is the size of your jar, and perhaps at least 1 cm (½ in) thick. Give them a cup of liquid and good instructions and support.

MOULD TROUBLESHOOTING
What happens if you get mould? People often mistake the lovely film that starts growing on top of their brew for mould. Sometimes it grows in an uneven pattern, heavy in one part and thin in another, which is fine. But if you are getting coloured patches, or furry growth that is obviously a mould, you'll need to toss your brew and start again. And consider why this happened.

You can grow mould:

– if you didn't have enough starter kombucha ratio to fresh tea. The pH needs to be low enough to keep unwanted growth away.

– if the temperature is too cool. If the brew ferments too slowly, the pH won't drop fast enough to keep the unwanted fungi away. Sometimes, humidity can be to blame, so ensure there is airflow.

– due to lack of airflow. Sometimes, your environment is to blame. Your brew should be in a place that is airy. That means a place you'd like to be in: fresh air, with some flow, and without other moulds or air pollutants. If you have mould in your house, it can quite easily find its way into your brews. For good or bad, there are yeasts floating around everywhere, and the wrong ones can find their way into your brew. If they aren't overpowered, they may grow.

– if there was mould on an ingredient. Tea is often the culprit. Washing it with one or two quick rinses of boiling water is a good habit before it steeps in the boiling water for brewing.

– due to water quality. If you are worried about water quality, then my method of pouring cool water into a tea concentration won't work – you should boil it all together when making the tea.

– if you get a SCOBY that has been stored in a refrigerator. You'll likely get a good enough brew for about five rotations before a mould joins in, and by then it's too late – don't blame yourself. Do make sure to get your SCOBY fresh and straight from a brew.

While mould is rare, it happens sometimes and is one reason to collect SCOBYs in another jar just in case. If mould forms on your SCOBY, you should throw out the entire batch, SCOBY and all. This won't matter if you have some spare. Simply make a half batch and take out the bottom layers of the SCOBY and add to the new jar. Let that sit, covered with cloth as usual and just allow it to grow. When the liquid is low, make some sweet tea and, once cooled, pour that into your jar just to give the SCOBY something to eat. More should grow until the jar seems quite full. They could sit like that for a year without much attention, at which point you may want to dispose of most of them and start again with one from near the top.

BELOW: THE 'MOTHERS GROUP'

VINEGAR

Another thing that has a SCOBY and grows pretty wild is vinegar. You probably already use vinegar in dressings, to pickle things, to brighten up dishes, or to poach an egg. Many people are having a splash of it every morning as a health tonic. There are indeed many ways and reasons to infuse vinegar: for flavour, or as a way to get the nutritional benefits from a herb, for example. You can also drink it in a cocktail, in a spritz, sweetened as a shrub or enjoy it watered down.

Vinegar can be found throughout history in many forms. I am particularly interested in the rich, aged rice vinegars from Italy, or a clay pot aged rice vinegar from Taiwan, or the well-known fruit and sweet potato vinegars I've had in Japan and Korea. You can easily start making vinegars from other bases or ingredients in this book, and from things you may have in your kitchen. Malting grain or growing kōji will also help you on your vinegar-making journey. But first up: how to make vinegar from your leftovers.

VINEGAR FROM WHAT YOU HAVE

Fermenters and home cooks would be lost without vinegar in their repertoires. There's something about the tangy and acidic kick of vinegar that lifts a dish, a sauce or dressing, or a drink. It's an interesting process of alcohol being further fermented by acetic acid. It doesn't need to be difficult, particularly if you already have wine or mead on hand, for example. During your fermenting life you'll probably make plenty of vinegar by accident, simply by leaving a brew too long. Mead makes a lovely honey vinegar, as does sake and wine. Fruit can be gathered and left to ferment with water and some sugar to get a vinegar. At one stage, I had a lot of kombucha vinegar around because I ambitiously made brew after brew, forgetting it each time (okay, not forgetting; knowingly ignoring it). I ended up putting the various kombucha or jun vinegars into catering-size squeeze bottles for my girls to rinse their hair with in the shower. It makes for shiny hair (and may also be a lice deterrent).

APPLE SCRAP VINEGAR

Apple scraps – the peels and cores – can be added to a jar to make a light vinegar for drinking, to use in mustards and sauces, and as a cleaning agent. It works well in Four thieves vinegar (page 175) and Fire tonic (page 173). It's not suitable for pickling as the pH might not be low enough.

Apples are covered in the best kinds of hungry yeasts and form the basis of the beautiful wild Basque cider on pages 120–2. It's quite easy to amass the scraps if you've done some baking or stewing.

Choose a jar based on the quantity of apple scraps – you'll want to fill a jar at least halfway. Clean and sanitise the jar really well with boiling water. Add the scraps, add water to fill the jar and add some sugar – just a bit, roughly ½ cup sugar (brown, raw or white) per litre (34 fl oz/4 cups) water. Cover the jar with a cloth and secure it with a rubber band. Leave it for a few days. It will start to ferment and become fizzy.

There are two options from here: you could strain out the apple bits, bottle the liquid and let it sit to make a lively, slightly alcoholic fizzy cider, a good option if you had a lot of apple in there. Taste before you lid the bottle – it may need another teaspoon of sugar or so to pick it up. Alternatively, if you want to make vinegar, allow it to sit for about 2 weeks before straining out the solids. Pour the liquid back into the jar, cover with a cloth and leave for another 2 weeks. It might slowly form a SCOBY on the surface, which is good! You can let it sit for months, tasting along the way. Remove the mother, strain and bottle. To flavour, add your choice of fresh herbs to the bottle.

PLUM VINEGAR

This is a great way to use up plums when you have a glut.

Place 1 kg (2 lb 3 oz) whole plums into a 1 litre (34 fl oz/4 cups) jar – stems removed and stem-side down. Push them down, cover the jar with a cloth and secure with a rubber band. Keep the jar at room temperature and keep an eye on it. You should push the fruit down and stir it after a few days, then daily until it becomes fizzy. As the fizz lessens, you won't need to stir it as often – just keep an eye on it, and after about 3 months, strain it. Use a strainer lined with cloth and gather the plums together, squeezing out all the juice. Bottle the vinegar. You can age it or use it straight away.

If you have a haul of blackberries, they also make a beautiful vinegar. Follow the method above. Use 200 g (7 oz) sugar for 1 kg (2 lb 3 oz) berries.

VINEGAR FROM WINE

For this you need wine (see Note), but you also need some raw vinegar to get things going – unless you have a vinegar mother already. A ratio of 3 parts wine to 1 part vinegar works well.

Pour a bottle of wine (750 ml/25½ fl oz/3 cups) into a jar, add 125 ml (4 fl oz/½ cup) raw vinegar and 200 ml (7 fl oz) water. If you have a vinegar mother, use it instead of the vinegar and water. Cover the jar with a cloth and secure tightly with a rubber band. Store it in a warm, dark place and leave for a few months – eventually a mother will grow. Now strain out your vinegar to bottle or age, transferring the mother to another batch. I highly recommend a continuous brew: take out half of the vinegar and just add wine until you reach the original amount to start a new batch. This will ferment faster.

NOTE: If you are using a high alcohol wine, you should water it down by almost half. A preservative-free wine will take less time than one with additives.

OXYMEL – A HONEY VINEGAR

This is an ancient herbal healing blend – the name literally blended from Latin *oxy* (acid) and *mel* (honey). Used throughout time, particularly in the Renaissance, oxymel has been experiencing its own comeback in bars, herbal dispensaries, restaurants and homes: it's a drink, a tonic, a mixer, an elixir. And it's incredibly easy to make. Raw vinegar and raw honey meet, usually in a 1:1 ratio, to cover a bed of herbs. For more powerful or bitter flavoured herbs you might want to make it sweeter with twice the amount of raw honey.

Flavour combinations abound for oxymels: what herbs do you have, what's looking good, what do you need it for? I choose cold infusion for

this. If you need to heat the botanicals to elicit more flavour, perhaps do that first with some of the vinegar, but since heating kills the life we are trying to hold onto, I'm inclined to keep things cool.

I usually make this vinegar in small 250–500 ml (8½–17 fl oz/1–2 cups) jars. I fill the jar about halfway with the herbs and then pour the honey over the top, followed by any raw vinegar – perhaps kombucha vinegar, apple-cider vinegar – measuring by eye. This is a great way to use up the rest of a bunch of herbs. I also love using some of the flowers from the herbs as they are usually a bit gentler than the leaf itself – borage, oregano, thyme and broadbean flowers are delightful.

I'm fond of the combination of half a jar of borage flowers, a borage leaf or two, a few sprigs of rosemary and yarrow, topped with the liquids. This little threesome is said to bring courage and help the heart.

Take … no, enjoy this in a shot glass, diluted in hot water, to sip on, mixed in a drink, as a dressing, in rice for sushi – it just depends on what you flavour your oxymel with, of course.

Infuse

INFUSE

IMPARTING FLAVOUR

In crafting wild drinks, it's good to have a handle on how best to extract flavours. This chapter is just that: infusions, in water, syrup or alcohol. Infusions like these are a fabulous way of extracting nutrients and imparting flavour, and are part of an old and far wider library of methods.

How you choose to capture and preserve your flavour will depend on its end use – are you going to drink it, or use it as a second ferment flavour? Will you use it instead of water? How you intend to use or enjoy it must be considered as well as how the ingredients will react – perhaps hot water steeping is enough; maybe it would be better drawn out in sugar or alcohol. It may just be a matter of trial and error for some ingredients, but it is good, then, to have a few different methods in mind when you are trying to make the most of what's at hand.

In relation to your other ferments and brews, particularly for second ferment flavours, it is sometimes more practical to capture a season and hold it for later by making a syrup.

An infusion is a broad category and refers to any preparation, be it plant, bark or root, steeped in a medium such as water, alcohol, honey, vinegar, oil or syrup.

JUJUBES SOAKING IN HOT WATER.

COMMON WAYS OF INFUSING

Decoctions tend to use heat, usually boiling, to help break down plants and herbs, most commonly the tougher, woodier parts: bark, roots and stems, for example. They require heat and time. You often drink these warm and savoury, like a soup, but can also serve them cool.

A tincture is an extract made by grinding or chopping fresh or dry herbs into small pieces and steeping them in a water/strong alcohol solution or glycerine for 1–4 weeks. They are usually made for medicinal purposes and are a concentrate for that reason, but are also a great tool in cocktails to enhance and mix flavours.

Distillation is the process applied to grain and fruit-based drinks that have already undergone alcoholic fermentation. The spirits that result are high in alcohol, and in this book, we use them to make some liqueurs by steeping and adding syrups. This style of infused alcohol has been enjoyed and employed before and after meals to aid in digestion, to calm the nerves or to lift the spirit, using herbs and other botanicals known for their beneficial properties. Distilled alcohol is also a great medium to preserve in or to extract flavours for use, as with vanilla, for example.

Infusions have long been made to calm or excite, amuse or invite, or even to medicate (drink only a little for that!) and allow you to serve or save a season in a bottle. They can be pretty intense as well and quite strong. There is a reason the traditional glasses made to drink an aperitif or digestif are so tiny. Should you be new to making drinks, infusions are a good place to start.

PANDAN AND LEMONGRASS WATER

Prep. 5 minutes | Infusion time: 5-10 minutes |
Equipment: 2 L (68 fl oz) bottle or jug, cloth (optional)

I am an official fan of pandan in drinks, but it is also a common ingredient in baking and cooking, is used as a green food colouring, to keep bugs away and for its healing properties – one of which happens to be aiding digestion. It has such a beautiful flavour, but at first, I did not take to it when I was a teen living in Malaysia; decades later, Palisa Anderson served it to us at Boon Luck Farm during our tour with Sandor Katz, and the delightful memory still lingers.

I've included this lovely thirst quencher here as an example of a simple water infusion, but it would also make an excellent first ferment for water kefir (page 142), or a base for a wild soda (page 112) or ginger beer (page 131), for example.

INGREDIENTS

2 litres (68 fl oz/8 cups) water
3 lemongrass stalks, outer leaves
  removed
5-10 whole pandan leaves
115 g (4 oz/½ cup) brown sugar
  (see Note)
ice, to serve

Bring 1 litre (34 fl oz/4 cups) water to the boil in a saucepan. Bruise the lemongrass stalks a bit, then roughly chop, along with the pandan leaves. Add to the saucepan and boil for 5 minutes. Reduce the heat and simmer for 15 minutes with the lid on. Remove from the heat, strain out the solids and add the sugar, stirring until dissolved. Add the remainder of the water and strain again through a cloth if needed. Pour into a bottle or jug and refrigerate.

Serve icy cold.

NOTE: You could use coconut sugar or palm sugar.

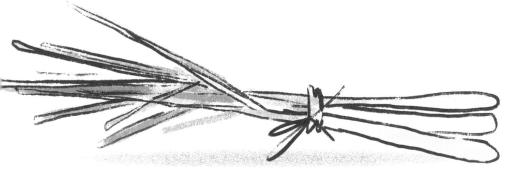

VINEGARS AND TONICS

When you ferment drinks for a while, there's a chance you'll start to make – often by accident – a variety of vinegars. See page 160–3 for more on making vinegar.

After tasting the most gorgeous fruit- and herb-infused vinegars in many parts of Asia and Europe, I was inspired to try my own, quicker-infused versions. I also find the traditional uses for infused vinegars quite appealing – and appetising.

SHRUBS

A shrub is essentially a herb- or fruit-steeped sweet vinegar that you can enjoy drizzled like a dressing or added to sparkling or flat water, same as a cordial. It works as a mixer in a cocktail too. This is an age-old way of preserving the flavours of fruits and other botanicals. Sweet and tangy shrubs are a great way to host a herb or to intensify a desired flavour. If you make a very good batch, you'll find it's good just enjoyed over ice.

Herbal shrubs can be made and imbibed as medicinal tonics, and many traditional shrubs are based on herbs, roots, barks and specific plant concoctions and were sipped with the purpose of healing.

You can make a shrub by cold infusion or by cooking, depending on the ingredients and state of the fruit, or how difficult you feel the flavours will be to pull out. Very sweet and soft fruits tend to impart flavours readily compared to roots, for example. Tougher ingredients will benefit from heat and time. You can use any vinegar for shrubs.

The basic ratio is 1 part fruit, 1 part sweetener, 1 part vinegar.

COLD INFUSION SHRUB

Prep. 10 minutes | Infusion time: 2-5 days | Equipment: 500 ml (17 fl oz) bottle or jar, muslin (cheesecloth)

INGREDIENTS

500 g (1lb 2 oz) fruit
440 g (1 lb/2 cups) sugar
  (see Notes)
500 ml (17 fl oz/2 cups) vinegar
  (see Notes)

In a large bowl or jar, toss the fruit, plus any herbs and spices (see next page for flavour combinations) with the sugar to macerate. Sit the blend on a bench, covered with a cloth, for about 2–5 days.

Agitate or stir the fruit each day. On the third day, strain the mixture by pressing into a sieve and setting aside the fruit pulp (see Notes). Taste for sweetness. Add approximately an equal amount of vinegar to the syrup, pouring, stirring and tasting as you add in increments. If you sat the macerating fruit out long enough, it may have a degree of tartness about it already, so do be sure to add the vinegar to taste. When you are happy with the shrub, simply pour it into a clean bottle or jar and keep it in the fridge. It should be fine there for a few months.

NOTES: White or raw sugar will allow fruit flavours to shine through, but some sweeteners carry flavours worth considering, so don't be afraid to experiment with them. I've found mild, gentler vinegar varieties – brown rice, coconut or champagne – work really well in a shrub, but I've tried all sorts. See Note below.

If you are using citrus fruit, peel it first and vigorously massage the peel in the sugar to release the oils, then add the chopped pulp. The fruit pulp can be used to make a compote or in a wild soda (page 112–15).

COOKED SHRUB

Start with equal parts sugar and water to make a syrup, stirring over a low heat until the sugar is dissolved. Add your chopped fruit and simmer for about 10 minutes, or until the syrup is the colour of the fruit. Add the vinegar in small amounts, tasting as you go, and return to a simmer. Leave to cool, then strain out the fruit and bottle the liquid. Store in the fridge.

FLAVOUR COMBINATIONS

- strawberries and fresh basil; white sugar; red wine vinegar and a splash of balsamic vinegar

- blueberries and bay leaf; honey; apple-cider vinegar

- plums sprinkled with matcha and red peppercorns; rice malt syrup; shiso vinegar

- blackberries and sage; raw sugar; champagne vinegar

- orange, cloves, pinch of pu'erh tea; white sugar; champagne vinegar

- blood plums and star anise; brown sugar; white-wine vinegar

NOTE: These will also work well (without the vinegar) in second ferment kombucha and water kefir or syrups.

FIRE TONIC

Prep. 15 minutes | Infusion time: 4 weeks |
Equipment: 2 L (68 fl oz) jar, muslin (cheesecloth), bottles

A fire tonic is a throat hitting, mouth-awakening vinegar-based folk medicine. It is easy to make. The ingredient list below is pretty extensive, but if you don't have a few of the ingredients, just leave them out or replace them with something similar. Horseradish, garlic and ginger are the must-have ingredients here, so don't omit those. You can adjust how spicy you'd like it – but it's called fire tonic for a reason. You can take a tablespoon of this by itself, dilute with a little water, or add a splash to cooking.

INGREDIENTS

approx. ½ cup fresh horseradish,
  grated (or preserved)
5 cm (2 in) piece fresh ginger,
  chopped
12 garlic cloves, peeled and
  crushed
1 onion, roughly chopped
juice and zest of 1 lemon
3-5 chillies (see Note)
2-5 large slivers of orange peel
3 small rosemary sprigs
5 cm (2 in) piece turmeric,
  chopped
2 tablespoons black peppercorns,
  crushed
2 litres (68 fl oz) apple-cider
  vinegar
1 tablespoon raw honey

Add all the ingredients, except the honey, to the jar, pouring the vinegar over last. Stir to combine, cover with a cloth and secure with a rubber band. Store the jar in a cool, dark place for about a month, checking and agitating it every few days.

Strain into a jug. Add the honey and stir to combine. Strain again into a bottle, using a funnel with a coffee filter, then shake to blend. Let sit to infuse for a few days before using. It's good to have a swig or shot glass a day, especially when you feel a cold coming on. This will keep for months unrefrigerated, but once you open your bottle to use, it's probably better to refrigerate.

NOTE: I like to use a mixture of chillies – green and red, fresh and dried.

FOUR THIEVES VINEGAR

Prep. 10 minutes | Infusion time: 10 days |
Equipment: 2 L (68 fl oz) jar, bottles

The story behind this vinegar is that during the Black Death, four men were raising havoc and ransacking houses that had been left empty, their occupants lost to the plague. The men remained healthy and appeared immune even through their punishment, which was to collect and bury the dead. They claimed this vinegar mixture was their secret potion, and they were forced to make the recipe public.

This can be used as you would any culinary vinegar, and also works for your home – spray it around the house to rid it of 'negative energy', spritz it on your face and body as a skin tonic (dilute 1 part vinegar to 2 parts water) or use it as a household cleaner (dilute 1 part vinegar to 1 part water). You may also like to take a teaspoonful as a tonic for good health. This is a useful elixir to decant into small bottles to give to friends, particularly when there is something going around.

INGREDIENTS

- 2 tablespoons each of fresh lavender, sage, rosemary, mint, marjoram, thyme
- 4 garlic cloves, peeled and crushed
- 2 tablespoons each of anise hyssop, pink peppercorns, juniper berries (all dried)
- 1 litre (34 fl oz/4 cups) white-wine vinegar, apple scrap vinegar (page 161) or apple-cider vinegar

Roughly chop the herbs and place in the jar with the rest of the ingredients. Lid and let infuse for 10 days, agitating now and then. Strain, then bottle.

JAMU

Prep. 10 minutes | Infusion time: 30 minutes; 2-4 days if adding a ginger bug (see Note) | Equipment: muslin (cheesecloth), bottles

You wouldn't go for long in Bali without seeing this powerful bright yellow tonic. With roots in Ayurvedic medicine, jamu is said to go back thousands of years as a medicinal brew. As with all traditional drinks, recipes differ for each maker, but it will always be centred around fresh turmeric, joined by other roots, such as ginger, and bark, such as cinnamon, plus flowers, seeds, leaves and fruit.

It's imperative to source fresh turmeric, but don't fret about the other ingredients – bringing it down to the basics of turmeric, ginger, a sweetener and something sour is fine. I generally only peel ginger and turmeric if a good scrub doesn't clean it or if it's a bit old.

It's a gorgeous vivid tonic, something to sip as is or dilute. You may like to further sweeten it with honey. Enjoy cold, in a little shot glass or on ice in larger glasses.

INGREDIENTS

```
2 jujubes (Chinese dates)
1 litre (34 fl oz/4 cups) water
150 g (5½ oz/¾ cup) fresh
  turmeric root, roughly chopped
30-50 g (1-1¾ oz) fresh ginger,
  skin scraped, roughly chopped
5 black peppercorns
2 tablespoons tamarind paste
1 cinnamon stick
2 teaspoons coconut sugar
juice of 3 limes
```

Soak the jujubes in a cup of the water while preparing the other ingredients. Chop the jujube, turmeric and ginger and blitz into a paste in a blender with the soaking water and peppercorns. Pour the turmeric puree into a small saucepan and add the remaining water, tamarind paste, cinnamon stick and coconut sugar. Simmer gently for about 30 minutes with the lid on until the sugar has dissolved and the mixture is aromatic. Cool and add the lime juice.

Strain into a bottle and seal. Refrigerate and enjoy.

NOTES: If you don't have a blender, just finely chop the ingredients and cook a bit longer (perhaps 45 minutes), then strain out the solids. To ferment, make a ginger beer mother (page 130) and add to cooled jamu. Leave it in a jar, covered with a cloth secured with a rubber band, in a warm room for 2–3 days, checking daily and agitating or stirring regularly. Bottle, sit out to carbonate, and refrigerate.

SYRUPS

Syrups are a very easy and reliable way of preserving a flavour for later, and having a few at hand will make your drink-flavouring life easier. Add to a second ferment of a kombucha, water kefir or jun, make into a shrub, pour to flavour a glass of milk kefir, over yoghurt or porridge. Syrups are also great when we don't have any 'buch or kefir in the fridge to use with the home soda water maker.

If you have a lot of something, particularly if it's getting on and not at its best, get your pan out and go for it. It's very soothing to stand by a cooktop, stir and lose yourself a bit. Syrups are also a lovely thing to give as presents: they pay tribute to a fruit or plant you have, or a time or place.

You can play with the water portion by using coffee, or Earl Grey tea for example, which works beautifully with other flavours. Adding leaves (fig, lemon, feijoa) to a syrup can change it dramatically and you don't need a lot, which works well for a foraging walk.

GENERAL HOW TO

– syrups have a 1:1 ratio of water to sugar

– use a heavy-bottomed saucepan with a lid

– add the water and sugar to the pan

– heat until the sugar dissolves, then add the botanical/spices/fruits, and simmer for a further 20 minutes, lid on

– turn off the heat, let cool slightly and then strain through a mesh strainer

– you might need to return the syrup to the saucepan and simmer for another 20 minutes

– pour into a bottle or jar, lid and refrigerate.

TONIC SYRUP

Prep. 15 minutes | Infusion time: 3 days | Equipment: 2 L (68 fl oz) jar, muslin (cheesecloth), bottles

INGREDIENTS

1 litre (34 fl oz/4 cups) water
zest of 1 lime
zest of 1 orange
3 lemons, juiced
1 grapefruit, juiced
2 stalks lemongrass, cleaned,
  topped and tailed and sliced (if
  dried, add to pot as is)
20 g (¾ oz) cinchona bark
  (preferably not powdered)
5 allspice berries
1 star anise
5 green cardamom pods
1 small stalks lavender
¼ teaspoon salt
250 ml (8½ fl oz/1 cup) sugar
  syrup (see recipe opposite)

Bring the water to the boil in a saucepan, with the zest and juice. Add all the other ingredients except the sugar syrup, cover and reduce the heat to simmer for 20 minutes. Let cool and pour the mixture into the jar. Seal. Keep it nearby and shake a few times a day for 3 days. Strain through a cloth-covered sieve into bottles. Add the syrup, then lid and shake. Store in the fridge.

NOTES: This may ferment a bit, which we're not afraid of – just make sure there is some headroom in your bottles. This will keep for months in the fridge. This is fairly strong and sweet and would do well as a second ferment for water kefir, but you can also serve simply with soda water. And then a splash of gin.

DATE SYRUP (SILAN)

Prep. 5 minutes | Equipment: muslin (cheesecloth), 1 L (34 fl oz) bottle or jar

Out of all the sweeteners, dates are the most nutritious. They are the Muslim equivalent of 'an apple a day' – instead of one apple, it is seven dates, and it's not the doctor we are keeping away but 'poison and witchcraft'. Seven a day is a lot of dates!

Dates were traditionally a sacred and important food source that was relied upon by overland travellers and sailors on long journeys; this was successful because dates are, by their very nature, already preserved.

I recently started making date syrup to add to milk kefir for flavour, and then added it as a second ferment in kombucha with lemon, and then started to add it to other brews, porridge, yoghurt and even kimchi paste in place of sugar. Indeed, this date syrup can be used to replace a sweetener in nearly all of the recipes in this book.

Because it has quite a long cooking time, I tend to do a big batch like this. It keeps in the fridge for a few months.

INGREDIENTS

```
1 kg (2 lb 3 oz) pitted dates,
   preferably Medjool
2 litres (68 fl oz/8 cups) water
```

Give the dates a quick rinse with boiling water. Seed and chop the dates, then put them in a saucepan with the water. Cover and bring to a boil. Simmer, uncovered for 2 hours, stirring now and again. Take off the heat and let cool.

Pour the mixture into a lined sieve over a large bowl – you will need to gather up the edges to form a bundle and squeeze it to get all the liquid out, so make sure the cloth is big enough. You may have to do it in batches, putting the pulp to one side and reserving the liquid each time. Squeeze the cloth, twisting and massaging, to get as much liquid out as you can – we are aiming for at least 1 litre (34 fl oz/4 cups) of liquid.

Pour the date liquid into a pan and simmer, uncovered, for 30–45 minutes, stirring frequently to avoid sticking. Reduce the syrup until it is thick enough to coat the back of a spoon. Take off the heat and pour into a clean bottle or jar. It will thicken further as it cools.

Store in the refrigerator, where it will keep for months. Bring it out of the fridge to make it more pourable.

VARIATIONS

- pandan: add 10–15 pandan leaves, chopped and pounded. Don't make too much at once of this beautiful green syrup as it is much better fresh.

- teas: add 4 tablespoons of loose-leaf tea. I'm very fond of Earl Grey.

- leaves: add a couple of aromatic lemon, orange, fig, bay, rose geranium, blackberry, strawberry, olive or artichoke leaves (crushed).

ELDERBERRY SYRUP

Prep. 5 minutes, plus soaking time | Equipment: bottles

With such a rich history in herbal medicine, this syrup belongs in the collection. Elderberries should always be cooked (or fermented) to eliminate the toxins in the seeds. If you have lots of fresh elderberries, dry them out first in your dehydrator, or simply lay them out on some newspaper. I add dried elderberries to teas and other brews and love to have them on hand, but the syrup is even more convenient and easier to impart flavour with.

INGREDIENTS

100 g (3½ oz) dried elderberries
1 litre (34 fl oz/4 cups) water
350 ml (12 fl oz/1 cup) brown rice
  syrup or honey

Put the berries and water in a saucepan and let soak for about an hour. Place over a medium heat and bring to the boil, then reduce the heat and simmer for 30 minutes, stirring frequently. Add the sweetener, stirring well. Remove from the heat, strain and cool to room temperature. Bottle.

BITTERS, INFUSIONS AND LIQUEURS

One of the most important ingredients in a liqueur is the ambience when you drink it. There are hundreds of liqueurs out there incorporating fruits, nuts, leaves and herbs, creams, honey – anything goes and has gone for a very long time. Liqueurs are strong, easy to make and designed to enjoy slowly in small glasses.

I rather like the idea of picking something in season – you don't need a lot of it – tucking it into a bottle to just wait, forget about it and remember it months later.

In many places, it is traditional to offer a herbal based liqueur after a meal as a digestive. A daytime drink to an Italian is fine and they do make a large range of them. A splash in your coffee? A nip after lunch? It rarely seems to be in excess, rather it is a celebration of flavours and good feelings … a little something that will slide down the throat, coating it long and luxuriously. A liqueur for freeing the words, opening the hearts and lightening the thoughts.

I'd like to say that these recipes were collected over time from my travels, meeting old aunts and grandmas along the way. The reality is that the recipes I have picked up are usually a result of having too much of a thing, or drinking something and wanting to make it myself and asking people who I think will know stuff. I don't take good notes and I primarily rely on my hand, eye and taste: a little more lemon, a little more sugar, less time. Sipping one of my liqueurs, I can't help but think about how I could perhaps improve it next season. Sometimes it's just so perfect … but maybe it's not the drink that makes it that way, but the occasion, you know?

A liqueur is usually made in two stages – adding the flavours into the alcohol first, infusing for about a month, straining, sweetening, then waiting again. A liqueur will store for years on your shelf or in your freezer, but it will take a month before it's ready to drink. So while you wait for it to work its magic, gather a range of small apothecary bottles and pretty glass bottles with little cork or glass stoppers. It's a very comforting sound when you bring a bottle out at night, pull out the stopper and pour into tiny glasses.

For the recipe base, I think it's best if everyone is able to use a loose equation and then peacefully claim the recipe for themselves:

botanical and alcohol + time + sugar and water + more time

While it's infusing, keep the liqueur out of direct sunlight, but not too out of your way as it's good practice to agitate it gently at least once a day at first.

It can be difficult to buy 95% alcohol for the purpose of making homemade liqueurs, so I tend to use a vodka or grappa. It's readily available, clear and quite flavourless, and it works a treat.

HAZELNUT LIQUEUR

Prep. 15 minutes | Infusion time: 6 weeks, plus 3 weeks |
Equipment: 1 L (34 fl oz) jar, muslin (cheesecloth), bottle

Making liqueurs like this feels like something my mum did in the '70s, but I think it is just an extension of my syrup stage. I like toasty flavours, so I roast the nuts, but you don't have to.

INGREDIENTS

250 g (9 oz) hazelnuts
60 g (2 oz/½ cup) cacao nibs,
  crushed
250 ml (8½ fl oz/1 cup) vodka
125 ml (4 fl oz/½ cup) brandy

For the syrup

55 g (2 oz/¼ cup) raw sugar
125 ml (4 fl oz/½ cup) water
1 vanilla pod, cut lengthways,
  seeds scraped

Toast the hazelnuts in a dry frying pan over a low heat. Leave to cool, then roughly crush with a mortar and pestle. Put the nuts, cacao nibs, vodka and brandy in a jar, seal and store for 5–6 weeks.

After the first infusion, make a syrup. Place the sugar and water in a small saucepan, simmer over a low heat until the sugar has dissolved, then cool. Add the syrup, vanilla pod and seeds to the liquor. Seal, then gently tip the jar to mix – it won't hurt to have a little taste at this stage. Store for another 3 weeks.

After 3 weeks, strain out the solids (see Note), then give the liquor one final strain through a coffee filter or lined funnel into a bottle. Done. Let settle for a few weeks, then taste. This ages well.

NOTE: You can store the drunken hazelnuts in a jar to put on top of your ama-zake (page 72) or serve with ice cream.

NOCINO

Prep. 15 minutes | Infusion time: 4 months, plus 1 month |
Equipment: 2 L (68 fl oz) wide-mouthed jar, bottles

The lovely thing about nocino is that you make it in late spring using soft
and fleshy green walnuts and set it aside, visit it in autumn, and finally
when the weather is cold and you're more in the mood for the darker,
bitter, herby-sweet liqueur – it is ready. Nocino definitely tastes like a
winter drink. It gets better with age and really comes into its own after
one year.

This drink is also steeped in a bit of folklore, both pagan and Christian,
which tells us the walnuts need to be picked by a barefoot expert woman
and left on the ground to catch the dew when the dark changes to light.
I just got mine from the grower in a bag, but it is a goal of mine to be an
expert woman.

My friend in nocino (and creative genius), Anthony Nelson, made a nocino
that we loved – out of honey, vodka and just-green walnuts. He also did a
late season batch with barely-green walnuts – almost too late but that was
delicious, too.

INGREDIENTS

20-25 green walnuts, quartered
zest of 1 lemon
zest of 1 orange
3 lemon leaves, crushed
1 bay leaf
1 clove
2 allspice berries
5-10 coffee beans
2 cinnamon sticks
2 vanilla pods
2 litres (68 fl oz) vodka or 95%
  proof alcohol (see Notes)

For the syrup
500 g (1 lb 2 oz) light brown sugar
500 ml (17 fl oz/2 cups) water

Combine the walnuts, zest, lemon leaves, bay leaf, clove, allspice, coffee
beans and cinnamon sticks in the jar. Split the vanilla pods and scrape the
seeds into the jar, then add the pods. Add the vodka. Stir, close the lid and
set aside for about 4 months.

After 4 months, make a syrup. Place the sugar and water in a small
saucepan and simmer until the sugar has dissolved, then cool. While it's

cooling, strain the walnut liqueur, transferring the liquid to your clean bottle or bottles, adding some syrup to each. Lid, then gently swirl to combine. You should let it sit for at least another month.

NOTES: You might wonder where you can get green walnuts – you have a couple of months leeway in early spring to look. The first time I got hold of them was through friends who had a walnut tree in their backyard; the year after, I contacted a walnut farm and ordered some. Easy.

The walnuts stain your skin for a while when you chop them, so you may want to wear gloves. No heat needed for this recipe either, so it's a lovely thing to do outside.

You'll love watching the colour as it changes from dark brown to deep bright green over the first week, then slowly changes back from deep bright green to dark brown.

If you're using stronger alcohol, double the water in the syrup.

YOU SAY LIMONCINO I SAY LIMONCELLO

Prep. 30 minutes | Infusion time: 3-4 days, plus 2 weeks | Equipment: 2 L (68 fl oz) jar, muslin (cheesecloth), bottles

As long as someone is saying it.

There are a lot of lemons in this recipe – or shells of lemons. This is a job for when the trees are dripping with lemons and you have already squeezed them for lemon curd or lemonade … or maybe they are golden lemons with less juice than they promise. No matter, you can take the peel and freeze the fruit to use in another ferment. Let's make good use of the peel.

Limoncello or limoncino, depending on what part of Italy you are in, loves to wait for you in the freezer for an unexpected moment after a lively, creamy, carbohydrate-rich lunch with wine and warmth and friends. Finish with a limoncello. Drink in the winter sun.

I have very fond memories of lunches ending like this with the school mums at the sweet Italian restaurant on the corner, a short walk from the kids' school in Brussels. We always said we wouldn't but then … why not? I'm so glad we did.

INGREDIENTS

300 g (10½ oz) lemon zest or
  slivers, from organic lemons
  (see Note)
1 lemon, juiced
1.5 litres (51 fl oz/6 cups) vodka
  (I use one at 40% ABV)

For the syrup
600 ml (20½ fl oz) water
6 small lemon leaves, crushed
  (optional)
600 g (1 lb 5 oz/2¾ cups) sugar

Wash the lemons well and let dry. Zest with a microplane if you like as it more easily avoids the pith, but long, carefully administered slivers are more traditional. You choose.

Add zest or slivers and lemon juice to the jar, pour over the vodka and seal. Put in a place out of the sun, within easy reach so you can shake the jar twice a day. Just look and shake, don't open. Leave for 3 or 4 days.

After the first infusion, make a syrup. Bring the water to a boil in a small saucepan and add half the lemon leaves, if using. Blanch them quickly (about 10 seconds) then remove. Add the sugar to the water and stir until dissolved. Cool.

Line a strainer, carefully strain the lemon zest or slivers from the liqueur, then add to the syrup. Taste – add more sugar or lemon juice accordingly. Pour into clean bottles, add a lemon leaf, if using, to each and seal. Let the limoncello rest for a minimum of 2 weeks. You need to put it into the freezer and pull that baby out when the timing is right.

NOTE: You'll need about a box of unwaxed organic lemons for this recipe.

FIG LEAF LIQUEUR

Prep. 30 minutes | Equipment: muslin (cheesecloth), 1 L (34 fl oz)
bottle

There is a beautiful big, very old fig tree that sits on the back of a piece of land in country Victoria my family owns. Sadly, 80 per cent of the farm burnt in bushfires that ravaged Australia recently – I took a sombre long trip down with my parents to see the devastation. I had been driving there, tummy sinking, selfishly and strangely obsessing about the fig tree, only to arrive and find it had miraculously survived. The fire had licked its periphery, but there it stood, proud among the ashes. We gave it a hug and I took a few leaves. It had worked hard to stay alive, I wanted to preserve that. I love that tree.

INGREDIENTS

```
5 dried fig leaves (see Note)
300 g (10½ oz) sugar
350 ml (12 fl oz) water
5 fresh fig leaves
375 ml (12½ fl oz) gin or grappa
```

Crush the dried fig leaves between your fingers, removing the stem. Combine with some of the sugar and grind with a mortar and pestle until broken up.

Combine the rest of the sugar and the water in a saucepan. Bring to the boil and add the fresh fig leaves. Let the syrup boil actively for 15 minutes, adding the fig sugar at the end to dissolve. Take the fresh leaves out and let the syrup cool.

Put a lined sieve over a funnel and strain the cooled syrup into your prepared bottle, catching the dried leaf pieces. Add the gin or grappa. Taste and add a bit of water to top up your bottle or if it's too sweet. While a few months will be enough to get an idea of what you have made, the leaf liqueurs do really well when left to age a couple of years.

NOTE: My post-bushfire adaptation of this recipe uses smoked fig leaves. It's not essential for this recipe but if you'd like to add a couple of smoky leaves, I've put a smoking method on the opposite page. If you smoke the fig leaves, you can add them to teas and other herbal infusions as well.

TO SMOKE LEAVES

I love a smoky flavour and you can add that in many ways, not just with the fig leaves but other leaves too, such as feijoa and blackberry.

Make sure to wash and dry your leaves well. Follow the instructions for your smoker, drying until brittle. Cool completely and store in an airtight container.

If you don't have a smoker, you can still fashion one quite nicely using aluminium foil, wood chips, a roasting pan and a rack that goes with or into the roasting pan.

Make a loose foil package containing the wood chips. Poke a few holes in it and place on the bottom of the pan. Place the rack on top, then lay the leaves on the rack. Put the pan onto heat, or light the chips directly. Wait for smoke, keeping a careful eye on the package so it doesn't go out, and when it's going well, close the lid or cover with aluminium foil. Smoke for 5 minutes – you may think it needs more or less – and turn off the heat. Make sure to fully extinguish the little fire you started: it can be deceptive, so maybe give the chips a cold bath before believing them. Your leaves are ready.

BLACKBERRY RATAFIA

Prep. 15 minutes | Infusion time: 3 weeks, plus 1 week |
Equipment: 2 L (68 fl oz) jar, bottle

A ratafia is a macerated fruit liqueur with additional flavouring often from
some kind of kernel base, such as apricots or almonds. In this instance,
we use almond essence. Keep the ratio at 1:1:1 fruit, sugar, vodka or other
clear alcohol.

INGREDIENTS

    1 kg (2 lb 3 oz) blackberries
    1 kg (2 lb 3 oz) sugar
    1 litre (34 fl oz/4 cups) vodka
    500 ml (17 fl oz/2 cups) water
    200 ml (7 fl oz) almond essence

Wash the blackberries, drain them well and leave to dry. Put the fruit into a
medium bowl, crush lightly, mix in the sugar and stir. Pour the fruit mix into
the jar and add the vodka. Lid the jar and leave to steep for about 3 weeks.

After the first infusion, add 500 ml (17 fl oz/2 cups) boiled water to the liquor
and stir thoroughly. Reseal and let rest for another week or so.

Add the almond essence, stirring well, then strain and bottle the liquor.
It will need at least a month to further steep and will get better with age.

PASTIS

Prep. 15 minutes | Infusion time: 5 days | Equipment: 2 L (68 fl oz) jar, muslin (cheesecloth), bottles

INGREDIENTS

1 tablespoon or large piece of
  dried licorice root
½ teaspoon dried angelica root
5 whole peppercorns
½ teaspoon fennel seeds
½ teaspoon aniseed, whole
¼ teaspoon coriander seeds
10 star anise
350 ml (12 fl oz) vodka

For the syrup
75–100 g (2¾–3½ oz) sugar
100 ml (3½ fl oz) water

Grind the licorice and angelica root, peppercorns, fennel, aniseed and coriander seeds with a mortar and pestle or spice grinder, but not too finely. Add the ground spices to the jar, together with the whole star anise and vodka. Seal well and shake. Steep for about 5 days (out of sunlight), shaking now and then.

After 5 days, make a simple syrup by combining the sugar (to taste) and water in a saucepan, and stirring over heat until the sugar has dissolved. Cool.

Strain the spiced vodka twice through a cloth-lined sieve, then bottle. Add the syrup to the bottle, seal and shake gently to mix. It should steep a full week before tasting. This will keep for months.

NOTES: I have also made this without the sugar syrup and enjoy it immensely.

How to drink? Usually before a meal, neat in a glass, with a little jug of water on the side to dilute, maybe with some ice. Mixing that together is my favourite part. Licorice root drinks are known to 'louche' a little and this can happen with homemade ones. It just means that when you add water, the drink can go a bit cloudy.

GRAPPA INFUSIONS

Grappa is an ancient, distilled drink made from the by-product of the leftover solids of wine. The solids are distilled with no water added and then aged for a minimum of 60 days. A good grappa will sit in wooden barrels, usually made of oak, mulberry, or juniper. You can buy some lovely grappa to enjoy straight, but it also comes in cheaper varieties that work as a wonderful medium to host and preserve a flavour in a liqueur.

The method is similar to others – first the infusion, then the syrup. Like all liqueurs, these will get better with age.

BAY LEAVES, BLACKBERRIES
AND PASTIS.

BAY LEAF GRAPPA

Prep. 10 minutes | Infusion time: 2 weeks, plus 2 weeks |
Equipment: 1 L (34 fl oz) jar, muslin (cheesecloth), bottle

This is an enchanting deep green. Add a dried artichoke leaf and perhaps a couple of fresh or dried angelica leaves if you have them.

INGREDIENTS

32 fresh bay leaves
3 rosemary sprigs
2 strips of orange peel
500 ml (17 fl oz/2 cups) grappa

For the syrup
100 g (3½ oz) sugar
100 ml (3½ fl oz) water

Wash and dry the herbs and orange peel. Add to a jar, top with the grappa and leave to infuse for 2 weeks, agitating once a day.

Make a simple syrup by combining the sugar and water in a saucepan and stirring over heat until the sugar is dissolved. Leave to cool.

Add the syrup to the liqueur and leave to infuse for 2 more weeks. Strain through a cloth-lined sieve and again into a bottle. Let age for a minimum of a month.

NOTE: Serve chilled and neat in small glasses to sip after a meal. For a delicious summery variation, make peach grappa. Simply replace the herbs and orange peel with 500 g (1lb 2 oz) fresh ripe peaches, peeled and stoned, and 1 teaspoon loose-leaf oolong tea. Follow the method above.

VERMOUTH

Prep. 30 minutes | Infusion time: 10-14 days | Equipment: 1 L
(34 fl oz) jar, muslin (cheesecloth), thermometer, bottles

Vermouth is an aromatised, fortified wine (red or white), once made to
save oxidised or 'off' wines by adding a stronger alcohol, such as brandy or
another distilled liquor, and flavouring it with all kinds of herbs and spices,
steeped for flavour and aroma. I think vermouth might be the ultimate
beginner potion.

For thousands of years, vermouth's forebear wormwood wine was a drink
of choice and was seen as a herbal elixir and a means to help digestion.
Wormwood is still a necessary ingredient in vermouth, indeed the name
derives from the wormwood wine in Germany called 'wermut'.

Although mostly known as an ingredient in a martini, a good vermouth is
delicious to drink without mixing, and we are aiming for something worthy
of that here. I think it's underrated as a drink on its own. It needs to be kept
in the fridge and consumed pretty quickly once opened.

INGREDIENTS

    1 teaspoon dried wormwood or
      2 dried sprigs
    6-10 dried chamomile flowers
    2 dried peppermint leaves
    5 juniper berries
    1 star anise
    5 cardamom pods
    1 tablespoon coriander seeds
    ½ teaspoon fennel seeds
    3 strands saffron
    pinch of dried sage
    shave of fresh nutmeg
    250 ml (8½ fl oz/1 cup) brandy or
      grappa (see Notes)
    2 × 750 ml (25½ fl oz/3 cups)
      light white wine (see Notes)
    100 g (3½ oz) sugar (see Notes)

Bruise the leaves and flowers a little, then crush the harder spices a little
with a mortar and pestle to open them up. Combine all the ingredients,
except the wine and sugar, in a jar. Shake it once a day for 10–14 days.

Strain out the solids with a cloth or filter paper-lined sieve and squeeze
to get all of the liquid out. You might want to strain with clean cloth again,
aiming to get the liquid as clear as possible. Leave it to settle before the
next step – perhaps for a couple of hours.

Pour the wine into a saucepan and add the sugar. Carefully add the herbal infusion, pouring slowly to hold back any sediment. Heat gently, stirring occasionally until the sugar has dissolved and the liquid reaches 70°C (158°F). Cool to room temperature.

Strain again, bottle and seal well. Age for at least a month before drinking, but it will improve further with a couple of years' shelving. Once opened, it needs to be stored in the fridge and enjoyed within a couple of weeks.

NOTES: For the fortification, you could use vodka. For the wine base, I most commonly use pinot gris, but it would work with a homemade or young wine.

You can adjust the amount of sugar, depending on whether you've used a dry or sweet wine and how sweet you like things. It will need at least 50 g (1¾ oz) sugar to avoid bitterness.

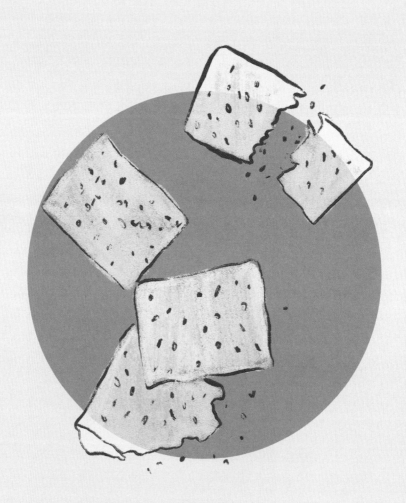

Enjoy

ENJOY

TRANSFORM YOUR LEFTOVERS

A satisfying and economical extension of
fermentation is using the leftovers to make
something else. This means that when a ferment
is finished, it is actually just another beginning.
Not all of these recipes are for eating and
drinking – some are for applying.

BASQUE CIDER CHICKEN

Use sagardoa apple cider (page 120) for this authentic and tasty chicken dish from the region. A big thanks to my Basque sister-in-law, Maitane Aruti, and her lovely kombucha-brewing mum for this recipe.

INGREDIENTS

```
2 tablespoons olive oil
1 whole chicken, cut into 8
  pieces (or 1 kg/2 lb 3 oz skin-
  on chicken legs or thighs)
2 teaspoons sea salt
1 teaspoon black pepper
6-8 garlic cloves, peeled
2-3 shallots, peeled and
  quartered
1 leek, white and light green
  parts only, sliced
3 thyme sprigs
500-750 ml (17-25½ fl oz) Basque
  cider (pages 120-2; see Note)
1 sprig tarragon
4 small, sweet apples, peeled and
  sliced
```

Heat the olive oil in a large heavy-bottomed casserole. Season the chicken pieces well and add them to the pan. Brown the chicken over high heat for about 6 minutes per side. Set aside.

Reduce the heat and grate three of the garlic cloves into the pan, adding the others whole. Add the shallots, leeks and thyme, sautéing until soft, about 5 minutes. Incorporate all the tasty brown bits stuck on the bottom of the pan. Return the chicken pieces to the pan and pour in enough of the cider to reach halfway up the sides of the chicken. Add the tarragon and apple slices. Put the lid on and cook over medium heat for about 25 minutes. Remove the lid and increase the heat to high, until the apples have softened, the liquid has reduced and the chicken is cooked through. Check the seasoning and serve.

Enjoy with a fresh green salad and some crunchy bread to mop up the sauce. A bottle of cider or Rioja would be lovely alongside.

NOTE: Any good apple cider will work in this recipe.

SAKE LEES (SAKE KASU)

Prep. 1 hour | Fermentation time: 4 hours, plus 6 hours |
Equipment: 1 L (34 fl oz) jar or bottle

Sake lees is the fermented grain residue from making sake. There are so
many uses for this leftover mash that it is also sold as an ingredient in its
own right. Look online or in a store that stocks Japanese food.

AMA-ZAKE FROM SAKE LEES

INGREDIENTS

    200 g (7 oz/1 cup) grains such as
      pearl barley, millet, quinoa,
      white or brown rice
    700 ml (24 fl oz/3 cups) water
      (for cooking the grains)
    450 g (1 lb) sake lees
    200 g (7 oz/1 cup) brown sugar
    700 ml (24 fl oz/3 cups) water

Boil the grains in the water as you normally would, in a saucepan or
rice cooker. Drain and transfer the grains to a jar and let cool to body
temperature. Stir in the sake lees, adding some of the water if need be.
The mixture should have a thick, porridge-like consistency.

Maintain the temperature of the mix at about 60°C (140°F) for 3–4 hours.
A yoghurt maker is ideal, but you can just immerse in a pot of hot water.
When the mixture becomes looser, add the sugar and the rest of the water.
Check the taste after 6 hours, bottle and chill.

PRESSED SAKE KASU

SAKE LEES BAKED CHEESECAKE

This baked cheesecake has the loveliest texture. It's moist, with a slight umami flavour from the sake lees, and it has such a delicate crumb. Your whole kitchen will be filled with the beautiful aroma of sake lees when you leave this on the bench to cool!

Sake lees can easily be added to any simple butter cake, shortbread or even to a bread and butter pudding. Wherever there's a dairy element in a recipe, such as cream, ricotta or cream cheese, try substituting 30–50% sake lees to lift the flavour.

INGREDIENTS

```
120 g (4½ oz) unsalted butter,
  softened
1 tablespoon vanilla extract or
  one vanilla bean, split and
  scraped
1 lemon, finely zested
200 g (7 oz/1 cup) caster sugar
4 eggs, separated and at room
  temperature
2 tablespoons lemon juice
240 g (8½ oz) almond meal
200 g (7 oz) ricotta cheese or
  milk kefir labneh
100 g (3½ oz) sake lees (loosened
  with a little water)
40 g (1½ oz) flaked almonds
icing sugar, to decorate
```

Preheat the oven to 160°C (320°F) fan forced. Grease and line the base and sides of a 20 cm (8 in) round cake tin.

In a large mixing bowl, beat the butter, vanilla, lemon zest and half the sugar with an electric mixer until pale and creamy. Add the egg yolks one at a time, beating well between each addition. Reduce to low speed and incorporate the lemon juice and almond meal in batches.

Combine the ricotta or labneh and sake lees in a small bowl, pressing the mixture gently through a fine sieve to remove any lumps. Fold the mix into the cake batter with a spatula.

In a separate mixing bowl, use an electric whisk to whisk the egg whites to soft peaks. Gradually add the remaining sugar, whisking continuously on high speed, until very stiff peaks form. Gently fold a third of the egg whites into the cheesecake mix, then gradually add the remainder until just incorporated. Take care not to overmix.

Pour the mix into the tin, smooth the surface with a spatula, and decorate generously and evenly with the flaked almonds. Press the almond flakes into the mix a little.

Bake on the middle shelf for 45–50 minutes. The cheesecake is ready when it's just firm to touch and has a slight wobble. Turn off the oven and leave the tin to cool for 15 minutes in the oven before transferring it to a rack. Allow the cheesecake to cool completely in the tin. Remove from the tin and dust generously with icing sugar.

SAKE LEES CRACKERS

These crackers were inspired by a recipe from the Terada Honke brewery in Japan. They have a lovely umami and a subtle cheese-like flavour to them. They are a great snack to whip up for any dairy-free guests.

INGREDIENTS

20 g (¾ oz) sake lees, plus enough
  water to make it into a paste
2 tablespoons olive oil, plus
  extra for brushing
100 g (3½ oz) flour (any type of
  plain/all-purpose flour)
1 teaspoon fine salt

Extra flavours (optional)

1 teaspoon black sesame paste
  (sprinkle with black sesame
  seeds at the end)
1 teaspoon tahini (sprinkle with
  sesame seeds at the end)
1 teaspoon honey (sprinkle with
  herbs of your choice at the end)
2 tablespoons ground pumpkin and
  sesame seeds (mixed through dry
  ingredients)

Preheat the oven to 180°C (350°F).

In a small bowl, massage the sake lees and water into a paste – this can take some work. Add the olive oil and mix to combine.

In a large bowl, combine the flour, salt and any extra flavours (if using). Add the sake lees mixture and combine to form a dough. You may need to add a little water to bring it together. Roll out thinly and brush lightly with olive oil. Sprinkle on the seeds or herbs (if using). Cut to the shape you like and transfer to an oiled baking tray.

Bake for about 10 minutes, then turn the crackers over. Reduce the oven temperature to 160°C (320°F) and bake for a further 10 minutes. Keep an eye on them – they cook quickly.

WHEAT-FREE SAKE LEES CRACKERS

This is a great way to use up nut pulp left over from making nut milk. The flavour combinations are endless. Try adding toasted nori with black sesame seeds, moringa leaf or spirulina powder to your next batch, or finely grate spent beetroot from your kvass (page 99) or carrots from the kanji (page 100) for extra colour. I've added a kimchi flavour here.

INGREDIENTS

    50 g (1¾ oz) sunflower seeds
    70 g (2½ oz) pumpkin seeds
    50 g (1¾ oz) sesame seeds
    1 teaspoon onion powder
    2 teaspoons salt
    50 g (1¾ oz) sake lees
    1½ tablespoons psyllium husks
    65 g (2¼ oz) nut pulp or almond meal
    1 tablespoon sesame oil
    2 tablespoons kimchi paste

Preheat the oven to 150°C (300°F).

Pulse the sunflower and pumpkin seeds in a blender until roughly chopped. Transfer to a medium bowl, add the sesame seeds, onion powder and salt and mix to combine.

Mix the sake lees, psyllium husks and nut pulp in the blender to combine. Add to the dry ingredients, along with the sesame oil and kimchi paste. Mix with your hand to form a dough.

Roll the dough thinly between two sheets of baking paper. Make sure to roll from the centre out to get an even thickness. Remove the top baking sheet and brush with sesame oil. Transfer to a baking tray, cut to your preferred shape and bake for 15 minutes. Carefully turn the crackers over, baking for a further 12–15 minutes. Keep an eye on them after about 10 minutes.

NOTE: If you don't have kimchi paste, add an extra tablespoon of sesame oil and use gochugaru – the chilli flakes needed to make kimchi.

LILY ENJOYING CRACKERS WITH KRAUT AND LABNEH KEFIR

SAKE LEES PICKLING BED (KASUDOKO)

One of the many beautiful things about fermenting or pickling in a bed like this is the feeling that you are re-planting something, sliding it back in to be transformed – enhanced and preserved this time. If you make sake, you will have the kasu left over to make this bed; if not, you can find it online and at speciality stores, or perhaps try to get in touch with a local brewer.

I've put sake in the recipe instead of mirin because it's hard to find a good mirin and the bed is safer with a touch of alcohol in it, particularly if you are marinating meat or fish. If you have 'Hon mirin' – genuine mirin – use it instead of the sake and sugar.

INGREDIENTS

```
450 g (1 lb) sake lees
50 g (1¾ oz) miso (use any miso;
  white is the most commonly used)
4 tablespoons sugar
1 tablespoon fine sea salt
50 ml (1¾ fl oz) sake
```

You'll need extra salt to apply to some of the vegetables to get the water out.

If you are using heavily pressed sake kasu (which is often sold in sheets), you may need to work it with a bit of sake first until it becomes pliable.

First make the kasudoko – the bed – by kneading the sake lees, miso, sugar and salt together until combined and the consistency of miso. Add the sake as you go – you might need more if the kasu is dry, or less if it is looser. Put the paste into your pickling container: this could be a zip-lock bag, a flat bowl, or a lasagne dish. Glass is good, plastic will work fine.

FOR CUCUMBERS

Sprinkle salt over whole cucumbers and leave them to drain. I don't weigh the salt, but as a guide, use about 2% of the weight of the cucumbers. Rub the salt into the skin of the cucumbers: we are trying to draw water from within the cucumbers before we put them into the bed itself. Let them sit for an hour, then wipe off the salt and slide them into the pickling bed, completely covering them with the kasudoko. Cover and refrigerate for a couple of hours or more, but no longer than 24 hours.

Scrape the kasudoko off with a knife or clean hands, leaving as much sake kasu in the dish as possible. To serve, slice the cucumbers on the diagonal and enjoy however you like. They go beautifully with just a bowl of miso and some rice.

FOR CARROTS

Wash and peel the carrots, cut on the diagonal and, without salting, just add the slices to the bed, making sure to cover them completely with marinade. Leave in the fridge for as little as 24 hours. After 4 days, they will have become true pickles. Wipe excess lees off and serve in a little dish.

FOR SALMON

Salt both sides of salmon pieces and set aside for 30 minutes to draw out excess water. Remove the salt with a paper towel and pop the clean pieces of fish into the bed, coating them thoroughly. Cover and refrigerate for 6–24 hours.

When you're ready to cook, be mindful that the sugars will be on the surface of the fish so it will burn easily – be careful. Place the fish on a baking tray lined with baking paper and grill for 10 minutes, turning the tray halfway through.

OTHER USES

IN A PESTO

Sake kasu tastes very similar to parmesan cheese in its umami-ness. There are no strict ratios here. Throw in some chopped greens (basil if you are going traditional), some oil, some sake kasu and blend away. Add some capers, a chilli and a handful of nuts or seeds. Blend it all up, tasting as you go – so delicious. Dollop as you would a pesto; it can also be enjoyed as a dip.

AS A FACE MASK

Yes, this is a thing! Sake kasu is full to the brim with active enzymes and all kinds of good things. There are some very successful skincare brands relying on the power of sake kasu. Try this mask – you may start making sake just to get the kasu. Seriously. You'll be very smooth and refreshed after this. This makes one treatment for the face and neck.

Mix 2 teaspoons sake kasu with 3–4 teaspoons rice water (see page 215) or plain water, massaging it together to form a paste. Add a squeeze of yuzu, lemon or honey. Apply to a clean face and neck, avoiding the eye area. Leave on for 15–30 minutes. Wash off with warm water.

STORING

The kasudoko bed will be fine to use and store in the fridge for about 6 months if you cover it. However, once you have used it for meat or seafood, do not use it for vegetables again. If it starts to smell too sour or becomes too runny, it's time for the compost.

SPENT GRAIN FROM BEER

High in protein, fibre, amino acids and minerals, low in calories. We call it spent grain – but you can spend it again in so many ways. Most of the sugars and starch have been left with the wort, and the grains are partially broken, which makes them easier to digest. They are too good to waste.

Wet grains need to be used within 24 hours, or they have to be stored in the fridge (for no more than a few days), frozen, dried or turned into flour. If left out, wet grains start to sour and ferment and become quite toxic.

Make sure to choose the right grain for the dish you are making. For example, wheat malt is great for bread and crackers, pale ale would be good for sweeter baked goods, and the darker malts are a great support for chocolate. Spent grains can be very chewy as they are rich in fibre; they will certainly add that earthy wholegrain texture that you probably don't want in finer textured breads. Spent grains are more on the 'energy bar' and earthy cookie spectrum – but have a play around.

Fresh-from-the-brew porridge is a good enough way to eat spent grains, and you'll notice that the smell of this fresh mash is perhaps more intoxicating than the beer will be. Its rather nutty texture is like a savoury Russian kasha and goes well with butter and salt, bitter greens, mushrooms and chopped roasted hazelnuts stirred though. Yum.

You can warm grains up as a porridge with butter, maple syrup and cinnamon. I did that to keep my nephew Tommy happy after a brewing session. He loved it so much we started wondering if it was okay … it is. He first just ate it 'for dinner' plain, just pulled and still warm from the brew, buttered and salted. The morning after brewing, I reheated it to make the sweet porridge, then we fed some to the chooks and froze the rest.

HOW TO DRY SPENT GRAIN
Keep spent grain in a container in the fridge for up to a week, or freeze until you are ready to work with it. Spread it in thin layers on a baking sheet and cook in a very low oven (80°C/180°F) for about 8 hours; if you prefer, you can do this in a dehydrator for about 12 hours at 65°C (150°F). The grain needs to completely dry out, so make sure to check in on it, moving the grains around gently from time to time and monitoring their progress. Take out of the oven when you think they are completely dry. Allow to cool. Store in a well-sealed container in your pantry.

FLOUR FROM SPENT GRAIN

Dry the grain, then pour a quantity into a powerful blender or appliance with a grain mill attachment. Grind. You may need to do this in small batches so the blender doesn't heat up. Store in a container as you would regular flour. Use this as you see fit – in waffles, breads and bars, in biscuits and bases, but keep in mind that it is coarser than fine flours.

Spent grain also works in:

- a chewy risotto or a pasta
- a crumb
- falafel or tabbouli
- recipes calling for wheat berries (both savoury and sweet)
- chicken or other pet food, such as baked dog treats (no hops for dogs, though: they are known to be toxic)
- compost: it's classified as green matter and will compost hot.

CINNAMON CRUNCH

This is similar to the activated buckwheat cereal known as buckinis, but more granola-like with malted beer grains. You can add dried fruit, nuts, seeds and spices. Plain, with lots of cinnamon, this is delicious atop yoghurt or smoothies, smothered in milk kefir, or anywhere you'd want extra texture or flavour. It's easy to prepare and keeps for at least a month.

INGREDIENTS

```
2 cups dried grain (see opposite)
125 g (4½ oz/½ cup) melted
  butter, ghee or coconut oil
170 ml (5½ fl oz/⅔ cup) maple syrup
95 g (3¼ oz/½ cup) coconut/brown
  sugar
¼ teaspoon sea salt
¼ teaspoon nutmeg
1 teaspoon cinnamon (and any
  other spices you'd like)
```

Preheat the oven to 150°C (300°F). Line a baking tray with a silicone mat or baking paper. Put the grain in a medium bowl. In another bowl, mix the other ingredients until well combined. Pour over the grains and mix until fully coated. Spread the mixture thinly and evenly on the baking sheet. Bake for about 45 minutes, mixing and turning the grains after 20 minutes. Let the grains cool completely, then store in an airtight container.

USES FOR SCOBYS

Once you are on your journey with kombucha or jun, you'll notice that the SCOBYs grow and grow and grow. Eventually, you'll have to tidy the collection up a bit. Before they get too old and slimy, try making some candy, jerky or even string – it is called eco-leather for a reason.

CANDY

This tastes like a sour apple sweet. Peel off a fresh and lovely looking SCOBY and slice it up into small pieces no bigger than 2 × 2 cm (¾ × ¾ in) – remember, it will rehydrate inside your mouth or tummy. I like to toss the pieces – they are already wet – in cinnamon or cardamom, for example. Place them in a dehydrator, set it at 38°C (100°F) and let dry. Check them and flip them when they need it; 24 hours should be plenty, depending on the thickness. You could get very creative with these and make fancy slivers that you dry to fit a glass edge to go with a drink.

JERKY

Slice the SCOBY strips into longer, thinner pieces than for the candy. Toss well in a savoury flavour that appeals to you – teriyaki, tamari, mirin, or ginger, for example – and dry as above. Serve with a beer or kvass.

ECO-LEATHER

Use a nice thin SCOBY for this: 2 cm (¾ in) is optimum. Peel it off carefully and dry it out flat. Rub it gently with a blend of beeswax and coconut oil a couple of times. You could cut these into coasters, dry them on top of a bottle or jar as a lid or make it into a bag. My favourite thing to do is to make it into string ties for my cloth covers.

MILK KEFIR FACE MASK

Milk kefir is not only good inside you, it also makes a fabulous creamy face mask. Decant a little milk kefir into a small bowl. Using a cotton ball or your fingertips, dab some gently onto your face. Leave the mask on for up to 15 minutes, then wash it off. It has a lovely enriching and softening effect. It makes your hands lovely and soft, too.

RICE WATER

When you wash and soak rice, keep the starchy soaking water; it is a precious resource and it would be a waste to pour all that goodness down the drain.

HOW TO

Let the rice water sit out, covered, and ferment for a day or two until it smells lemony and sour. Pour it into a large catering squirt/sauce bottle and keep in the fridge for when you need it. It will keep for a few days.

Use it ...

– as a hair rinse: pour over your hair after shampooing and conditioning; let it sit for a couple of minutes, then rinse well

– as a skin tonic (especially good for sensitive skin): rinse your face with it or spot treat with a cotton ball; either leave it on or wash it off – it's known to be great for acne

– to water pot plants or add to the compost or garden bed: the starchy water is a mild fertiliser and encourages beneficial bacteria

– as a rough rice beer (see page 73).

INDEX

RECOMMENDED READING

Brews
Hiroshi Kondō, *Saké*. Kodansha International, 1984.

Stephen Harrod Buhner, *Sacred and Herbal Healing Beers*. Siris Books, 1998.

Randy Mosher, *Radical Brewing*. Brewers Publications, 2004.

Craig Hughes, *How to Make Cider, Mead, Perry and Fruit Wines*. Spring Hill, 2012.

Emma Christensen, *True Brews*. Ten Speed Press, 2013.

Judith Glover, *Drink Your Own Garden*. Pavilion Books, 2013.

Jereme Zimmerman, *Make Mead Like a Viking*. Chelsea Green Publishing, 2015.

Marika Josephson, Aaron Kleidon and Ryan Tockstein, *The Homebrewer's Almanac*. Countryman Press, 2016.

Sandor Katz, *Wild Fermentation*. Chelsea Green Publishing, 2016.

Patrick E. McGovern, *Ancient Brews*. W.W. Norton & Company, 2017.

Pascal Baudar, *The Wildcrafting Brewer*. Chelsea Green Publishing, 2018.

Kōji
Kirsten K. Shockey and Christopher Shockey, *Miso, Tempeh, Natto & Other Tasty Ferments*. Storey Publishing, 2019.

Rich Shih and Jeremy Umansky, *Koji Alchemy*. Chelsea Green Publishing, 2020.

Vinegars
Bettina Malle and Helge Schmickl, *The Artisanal Vinegar Maker's Handbook*. Spikehorn Press, 2015.

Infusions
Guido Mase and Jovial King, *DIY Bitters*. Fair Winds Press, 2016.

Michael Harlan Turkell, *Acid Trip*. Abrams, 2017.

Selena Ahmed, Ashley Duval and Rachel Meyer, *Botany at the Bar*. Leaping Hare Press, 2019.

Garden and Herbs
Amy Stewart, *The Drunken Botanist*. Algonquin Books of Chapel Hill, 2013.

Food
Diana Henry, *Crazy Water Pickled Lemons*. Mitchell Beazley, 2002.

Pietro Demaio, *Preserving the Italian Way*. Self-published/Pan Macmillan, 2009/2021.

Barbara Abdeni Massaad, *Mouneh*. Interlink Books, 2018.

Drinks
Tom Standage, *A History of the World in 6 Glasses*. Walker, 2005.

ABOUT THE AUTHOR

Sharon Flynn is the founder of The Fermentary and one of Australia's leading authorities on fermentation; she was named a Melbourne Food and Wine Festival Legend in 2021 for her work and advocacy. Her bestselling first book, *Ferment For Good*, is beloved by aspiring and accomplished fermenters alike. Sharon draws on a body of knowledge established over more than two decades living in Malaysia, Japan, the US and Europe, and introduces readers to fermentation with warmth, charisma and wisdom.

GRATITUDE

To life – the life within and on and around us, always fluid and changing.

The matter you choose to ferment will change; sweet can turn savoury or sour, flat will become lively, light may become dark or bright, hard exteriors soft and luscious. Inside the vat – the less visible part, but the main thing – is all life, birth, growth and death, separation and transformation. Who is to say when it's ready, when it's at its most delicious, when to stop it, give up on it, cool it down? Fermentation is transformative no matter the substance, but the practice itself often brings about significant personal transformation of the fermenter. I've seen it over and over. Some people become spiritually intoxicated, hearts and minds captured, thirsty and deliciously curious. They get swept up, addicted. Perhaps their own microbiome was ripe to be taken over and seduced. Lucky, because there is enough to learn and love for a lifetime.

I am grateful for the patience and support I've had birthing this (COVID) book. To Jane Willson and Anna Collett from Hardie Grant Books, for the gentle pushes, and Kate Daniel for sorting through my work. To Mark Roper, who so calmly took the stunning photos, with Lee Blaylock making our work look beautiful. To Andy Warren, the illustrator and book designer.

For sharing dreams and ideas – support through hard times, hosting us for photo shoots (and for the best accommodation I can imagine) and growing my dream apothecary garden for more workshops – I am grateful to Sandy Cummins and Rob Roy of Acre of Roses. Thank you to Victoria and her team at Manteau Noir for the beautiful clothes for the shoot. To John Reid and the team at Red Beard Bakery in Trentham – thank you for making the cheesecake and for allowing us to shoot on your premises. To John Flynn, the 'wasbund' – still here – a sound ear and young spirit through thick and thin. To Willow and Ryder. To my loves Cheryl Maguire, Robyn Patton, Chiza Westcarr, Jackie Cammell, Melanie Bailey, Wendy Hargreaves, Petrina Baker.

To my little brother, Mark Turner-Arruti, who played with fermentation during a long lockdown in Spain and sent me recipes to try. To my big brother, Craig, for making beer and being a curious fermenter. To Tommy for loving my kefir. To my friend in sake and kōji, Melissa Mills, and my friends in fermentation, Anthony Nelson, Holly Davis, Andy Gott, Mandy Hall, David Zilber, Brad Leone and Sandor Katz. Also to Jung Eun Chae and Julia Mellor for support with my makgeolli recipe. To my favourite beer brewers, Gabrielle and Chris of Sailors Grave, for lending me their books and their time. For your interest and encouragement in what was a crazy hard year – the Studd family, Brigitte Hefner, Kirsten Bradley, Palisa Anderson, Jane Faulkner, Tony Tan, Matt Stone, Jo Barrett, Peter Gilmore. To all of the stores and restaurants who stock our ferments, and treasured customers who come into the cellar door and love what we do. We love it too.

A huge deep bow to my daughters, Isabella, Lily and Lucia – fluent fermenters, threading their gold all through this small business and the recipes in this book. We like to see each other thrive and alight with passion, but at times mine burns too bright I think. I'm both guilty and very grateful for how gracefully and generously all three bend for me. To my parents, for being tight and good and there for anything.

And to our ancestors; the people before us who experimented, shared, connected processes and their reactions, and who passed these skills on so we have them today.

And then: YOU, the whole curiouser and curiouser wide world that makes up our Ferm Fam. X
May you be captured by the magic, and may the microbes be transformative!

Published in 2022 by Hardie Grant Books,
an imprint of Hardie Grant Publishing

Hardie Grant Books (Melbourne)
Wurundjeri Country
Building 1, 658 Church Street
Richmond, Victoria 3121

Hardie Grant Books (London)
5th & 6th Floors
52-54 Southwark Street
London SE1 1UN

hardiegrantbooks.com

Hardie Grant acknowledges the Traditional Owners of the country on
which we work, the Wurundjeri people of the Kulin nation and the
Gadigal people of the Eora nation, and recognises their continuing
connection to the land, waters and culture. We pay our respects to
their Elders past and present.

 A catalogue record for this
book is available from the
National Library of Australia

Wild Drinks
ISBN 9781 74379 611 5

10 9 8 7 6 5 4 3 2 1

Publishing Director: Jane Willson
Project Editor: Anna Collett
Editor: Kate Daniel
Design Manager: Kristin Thomas
Designer: Andy Warren
Photographer: Mark Roper
Stylist: Lee Blaylock
Production Manager: Todd Rechner

Colour reproduction by Splitting Image Colour Studio
Printed in China by Leo Paper Products LTD.

The paper this book is printed on is from FSC®-certified forests
and other sources. FSC® promotes environmentally responsible,
socially beneficial and economically viable management of the
world's forests.